IN SEARCH OF

The
Battlefields
of Britain

Marc Alexander and Paul Abrahams

The
History
Press

Front cover

   Top: The magnificent statue of William the Conqueror in Falaise, the
   town of his birth.
   Bottom: The battlefield of Naseby.

Back cover

   Top: Statue of Robert the Bruce at Bannockburn, the scene of his
   greatest triumph.
   Bottom: The church of St Mary Magdalene, Shrewsbury, founded by
   Henry IV on the battlefield after his victory in 1403.

The authors would like to thank English Heritage
for their helpful assistance.

First published 2009

The History Press
The Mill, Brimscombe Port
Stroud, Gloucestershire, GL5 2QG
www.thehistorypress.co.uk

© Marc Alexander and Paul Abrahams, 2009

The right of Marc Alexander and Paul Abrahams
to be identified as the Authors of this work has been
asserted in accordance with the Copyrights,
Designs and Patents Act 1988.

British Library Cataloguing in Publication Data.
A catalogue record for this book is available from the British Library.

ISBN 978 0 7524 5191 6

Typesetting and origination by The History Press
Printed in Great Britain

CONTENTS

INTRODUCTION

Britain is rich in monuments that signpost her past but arguably the most evocative reminders of events that have shaped our island story are not man-made – they are battlefields. Unlike castles and cathedrals, they are not so obvious on the landscape and therefore an Ordnance Survey (OS) reference is given with each map on the following pages. While the standard reference is in six digits, allowing a point to be indicated with an allowance of 100m either way, battlefields very often covered several square km in area. For instance the line-up of armies at the Battle of Marston Moor stretched between the two villages of Tockwith and Long Marston – a distance of about 3km.

The object of this book is not only to give the location of battlefields but also provide a thumbnail description of the day's fighting – most British battles were over by nightfall - and explain their historical significance. For example, at first sight Bosworth Field is a piece of rural landscape, yet here when Richard III was betrayed and slain a royal house was ended after ruling for over three centuries. Supposing, as in the game of 'What if...', the king's allies had remained loyal there would have been no Henry VIII, no Bloody Mary, no Elizabeth I.

At first sight the quarrels between factions of royal houses can appear confusing, as with the Wars of the Roses, but a quick look at the genealogical tables at the back of the book will help to explain the violent disputes of the time.

One of the earliest descriptions of a battle fought in Britain was written by the historian Tacitus (*c*.AD 56–*c*.120) following the rebellion led by Queen Boudicca of the Iceni tribe against the Roman overlords. Following the death of her husband Prasutagus, tax collectors with a detachment of soldiers entered her royal residence claiming the late king owed Rome a great sum of money. According to Tacitus when the queen declared she could not pay such a sum 'Kingdom and household were plundered like prizes of war... as a beginning Boudicca was flogged and her daughters raped.'

In June AD 61 Suetonius Paulinus, the Roman Governor of Britain, moved two-thirds of his army to Wales to crush the Druids. The humiliated queen took this opportunity to raise a rebel army, which captured and razed Camulodunum (now Colchester). It then headed south burning Roman settlements on the way.

When the great force of Britons approached London the Romans left the city to its fate with the result it was destroyed and around 20,000 of its citizens perished. St Albans was the next to fall to the wrath of the Iceni queen. In August Suetonius brought his infantry down to confront the Britons. He took up his position at the mouth of a defile with a dense forest behind him and open land sloping away from him in front. Outnumbered ten-to-one he did not have enough legionaries to face the rebel battle line and was forced to split his force into three groups. So confident of victory were the Britons that they brought their families to watch the spectacle of a Roman defeat from a great semicircle of wagons.

Wave after wave of rebels charged up the slope to hurl themselves against the Romans' locked shields only to be repulsed. This was the pattern of the battle until the attackers were exhausted. Then the Roman troops began an inexorable march forward in wedge-shaped formations. This disciplined advance panicked the Britons but as they attempted to flee they found themselves hemmed in by their wagons. The battle became a massacre and according to legend Boudicca and her daughters committed suicide by poison.

Tacitus did not give the position of the battle and over the years a number of locations have been suggested. The authors believe the most likely spot is a field 2km north-west of Ambresbury Banks in Epping Forest where a local tradition claims that an obelisk marks the scene of the battle.

Another ancient battle relates to the legendary Arthur who, according to some early narratives, halted the Saxon invasion when the realms of myth and history merged at the beginning of the so-called Dark Age.

His greatest battle took place at 'Mons Badonicus', or Mount Badon, between Britons and Saxons. There are several ancient sources, all of which refer to this battle in which the leaders of the Saxons were Aelle and Aesc and the leader of the Britons was Arthur. Geoffrey of Monmouth, in his *Histories of the Kings of Britain*, gives a dramatic account of the action, which allows us some eight hundred years later to re-construct the scene.

Whether or not the leader was, indeed, named Arthur, most historians now do accept that the battle did take place in about AD 500, and there are five or so places with claims to the site, including Badbury Rings in Dorset, Bath, Baydon in Wiltshire and Strathclyde. That at Liddington Castle near Badbury, close to Swindon, appears to the authors to have the strongest claim and is included in this guide.

All photographs by the authors. Maps drawn by Paul Abrahams.

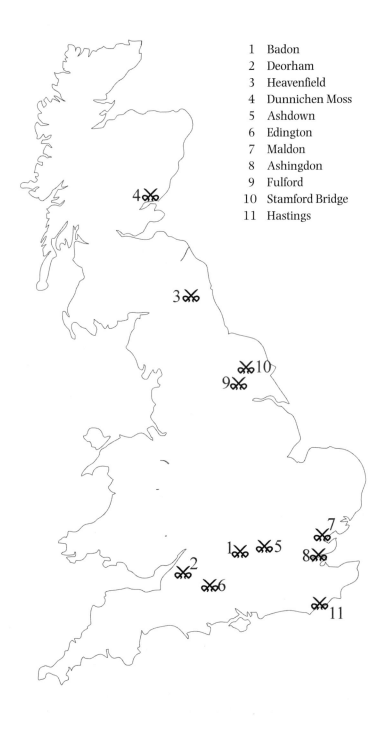

1 Badon
2 Deorham
3 Heavenfield
4 Dunnichen Moss
5 Ashdown
6 Edington
7 Maldon
8 Ashingdon
9 Fulford
10 Stamford Bridge
11 Hastings

INVASION AND SETTLEMENT

500-1066

From the departure of the Romans to the arrival of the Normans, the many invasions by such diverse people as Saxons, Angles, and Jutes were the result of a desire of these peoples to settle in a new country. Over a period of some 400 years (410–800), the native British were pushed west, and groupings of the invaders became kingdoms such as Deira, Bernicia, Northumbria, Mercia, East Anglia, Wessex and so on.

Battles took place between the native British and the Anglo-Saxons (Badon 500, Deorham 577, Heavenfield 633), between the new kingdoms and the Picts in the north (Dunnichen Moss 685), and even between the new kingdoms themselves, but by the end of the eighth century, 'the Saxons' or 'the English' had occupied virtually the whole of the country and were being identified as the true natives. There was, however, still no concept of 'England'.

Now there were new invaders – the Danes and Vikings – and battles were fought between these new invaders and the Saxons. Following Alfred's two major battles with the Danes at Ashdown (871) and Edington (878), Wessex became the most powerful kingdom in the country. The Danes, however, still retained a large area of the country in the north and east, and their position was strengthened after the Battle of Maldon (991).

Edmund Ironside of Wessex fought two battles with the Danish king, Canute, at Ashingdon (1016) and a year later at Deerhurst, after which England was divided between them, Edmund in the south and Canute in the north. When Edmund died in 1017 Canute became king of all England with the old kingdoms now converted to earldoms, each the stronghold of a particular family with a somewhat doubtful allegiance to the overall king. During the reign of Edward the Confessor (1042–1066), the Godwins of Wessex became the strongest family in the country despite a two-year exile in 1051–52, which did not lessen their hunger for ultimate power.

When Edward the Confessor died childless on 5 January 1066, there was no straightforward succession to the throne of England. Edward's younger brother, Alfred, had been murdered by Earl Godwin of Wessex and Edward had pledged the throne in 1051 to his cousin, Duke William of Normandy. Nevertheless, Harold, the son of Earl Godwin, and the strongest contender in the country, was crowned king. It was now a question of who would be the first to challenge his position. William was just across the Channel, waiting for a favourable wind to sail and invade, but Harold's brother Tostig and Harald Hardrada, King of Norway, who also had a tentative claim in his own right, made the first move. They sailed up the Humber and then the Ouse with an army of some 12,000 to threaten York. On 20 September 1066, Morcar of Northumbria and Edwin of Mercia met the invaders at Fulford, but were overwhelmed, and Harald and Tostig retired temporarily to Stamford Bridge to await hostages from the city of York.

Having heard of the invasion, Harold decided to march north immediately. He left London on or about 18 September and by 25 September had reached Stamford Bridge. His unexpected arrival surprised Hardrada and in the ensuing battle, Hardrada and Tostig were defeated and killed.

Harold had no time to rest. William had found his favourable winds and landed at Pevensey on 28 September. Harold returned south at high speed, leaving many of his experienced troops to follow as fast as they could. This rapid forced march enabled him to face William just north of Hastings at what is now the town of Battle on 14 October, but with a weakened force. The battle, the most significant ever fought on the mainland of Britain, lasted all day between two forces of roughly equal numbers, and eventually, with Harold killed, the Normans prevailed. William was crowned King of England in Westminster Abbey on Christmas Day 1066.

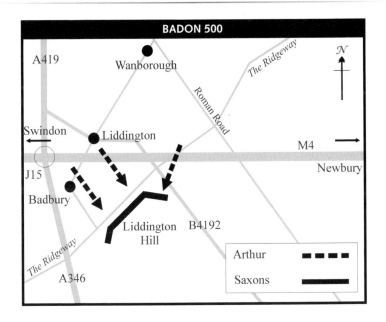

OS: SU195804

The village of Badbury is just off J15 of the M4 and the A419. Liddington Hill is about 1.5km to the south-east of the village. The Saxons from Sussex, Kent and East Anglia had probably come via the Ridgeway and the two Roman roads from the south and south-east, which meet just north of Wanborough.

The Britons had foregathered at Cirencester with its splendid Roman roads, and marched south-east along Ermin Street to Wanborough, while the Saxons had a defensive position hinging at their left upon what is now the village of Badbury and north-west of the Ridgeway with the possibility of withdrawing to a stronger position in their rear if necessary at Liddington Castle, an ancient fort. Their line followed the summit of a ridge with steep falls to the front and the sides. The Saxons were drawn up in wedge formations to neutralise the strength of Arthur's cavalry, which by all accounts was his main weapon. According to Geoffrey of Monmouth, the battle between the attacking Britons and the Saxons raged all day until evening without any advantage to either side. During the darkness, the Saxons withdrew to the hill fort of Liddington Castle with its very steep slopes. At dawn the next day, Arthur attacked again, this time with just infantry, and after another all-day battle eventually reached the top. Now he could bring up his cavalry via the eastern approaches and complete a notable victory, which would bring peace to the land for another fifty years.

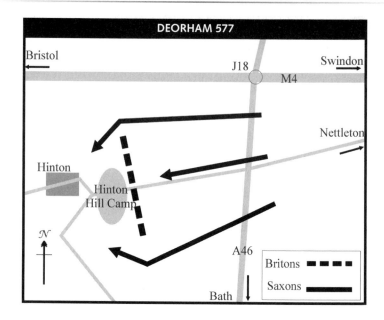

OS: ST745765

The general site is found by leaving the M4 at J18, taking the A46 south. Hinton Fort is a short way along the first turning to the right. The Saxons advanced from the direction of Nettleton, while the British were encamped on or near the hill fort of Hinton camp astride the trackway.

Between 552 and 577 the Saxons were gradually advancing north-westwards through Wiltshire, Oxfordshire and Gloucestershire. Their overall plan was clearly to push towards the Severn in an attempt to cut the country into two. In 577, a large Saxon army under Cuthwin and Ceawlin was approaching Deorham (the modern Dyrham) along the old trackway, where a combined British army led by the 'kings' of Gloucester, Cirencester and Bath were drawn up. An initial defensive position on a forward ridge was protected in the rear by the fortifications of the ancient hill fort of Hinton Camp. The pressure of the Saxon attack gradually pushed back the Britons until they were fighting with their backs to the old camp. Now the Saxons swept round on both wings and totally surrounded the Britons. It is recorded that all three British leaders, Commail, Condidan and Farinmail, lost their lives.

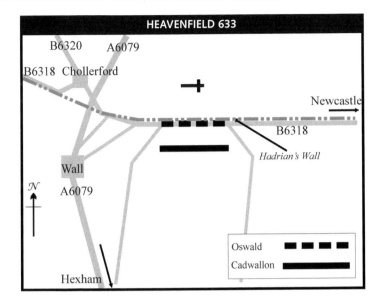

HEAVENFIELD 633

B6320 A6079

B6318 Chollerford

Newcastle

B6318

Hadrian's Wall

Wall

N

A6079

Oswald

Cadwallon

Hexham

The battle was fought about 2.5km east of the point where the A6079 crosses the B6318. Oswald had marched from Bamburgh and Cadwallon from York up the Roman Dere Street. There is a wooden cross, a chapel and a noticeboard beside the B6318.

In 616 Edwin became the first Christian king of both Bernicia and Deira, combining them into the single kingdom of Northumbria. His military strength allowed him to invade Gwynedd and conquer the Isle of Man. This, in turn, led to a counter-attack on Northumbria by a coalition of the kings of Mercia and Gwynedd. In 632 Cadwallon of Gwynedd and Penda of Mercia met and defeated the army of King Edwin at Haethfelth. Edwin was killed and the victors split Northumbria into its former parts of Bernicia and Deira.

In the period immediately following this defeat, the direct heirs of Edwin were also killed, leaving his nephew, Oswald, to attempt to regain the kingdom. Oswald had been raised in exile by Christian monks at Iona but now returned to take up the old kingdom of Bernicia.

In 633, he marched south from his capital of Bamburgh while Cadwallon marched north from York. They met at the Roman wall just north of Hexham. Oswald, a devout Christian, raised a large wooden cross as his standard and he and his men prayed together the

Roadside cross on the B6318 marking the site of the Battle of Heavenfield.

night before the battle. Although Oswald had the inferior numbers, his men were fighting both for their land and their religion.

After a fierce and bloody battle in which Cadwallon was defeated, Oswald raised a chapel on the spot where he had originally placed the cross and Northumbria was reunited once more. Archaeological evidence suggests that the battle ranged north and south of the wall.

The present chapel was built in 1717 on the same spot, and the battlefield has ever since been known as Heavens Field, or Heavenfield.

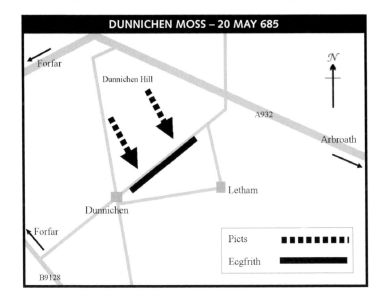

DUNNICHEN MOSS – 20 MAY 685

OS: NO510488

The battle was fought in the area between Dunnichen Hill and a loch which existed just to the north-west of the present town of Letham. The topography indicates that the two armies stretched along the line of a small by-road leading from the village of Dunnichen to the A932.

In 678, Ecgfrith, the leader of the Northumbrians, was thwarted in his dreams of southerly expansion by Aethelred at the Battle of Trent, the last battle between Mercia and Northumbria for over thirty years, and consequently turned his eyes to the north. The kingdom of Northumbria then stretched from the Humber to the Forth. In 685 he marched north against the Picts under King Brude Mac Beli. After retreating strategically, drawing Ecgfrith ever north into the Sidlaw Hills, the Picts turned against the Northumbrians on 20 May at Nechtans Mere, a loch which has since disappeared, but whose site has been identified as being between Dunnichen and Letham, south-east of Forfar. Here Ecgfrith was caught in a running battle and found himself trapped against the shore of the loch. His bodyguard stood fast to the end but eventually they were decisively beaten and Ecgfrith slain. The Northumbrians were driven back south, and that part of what was to become Scotland reverted to independent Pictish rule.

There is a monument at the church in Dunnichen, and a Pictish stone at Aberlemno which may refer to the battle.

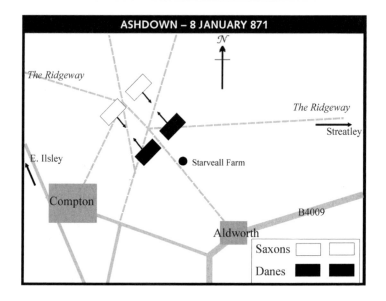

ASHDOWN – 8 JANUARY 871

OS: SU540815

The battlefield is 2km north-west of Aldworth (on the B4009) past the present farm of Starveall or can also be reached either by following The Ridgeway westwards from just north of Streatley, or eastwards from the A34 just 3km north of East Ilsley.

On 5 January King Ethelred of Wessex and his twenty-two-year-old brother, Alfred, had been forced by the Danes to retreat northwards from Reading and had reached Lowbury Hill about 1km north of The Ridgeway. The Danes, under their king, Bagsac, followed and camped within sight of the Saxons in the evening of 7 January at what is now Starveall Farm. The Saxons moved south to meet the Danes across The Ridgeway, and the two armies faced each other divided into two wings each. The Danish right was commanded by King Bagsac and King Halfden and their left by the Danish earls. The Saxons also formed into two columns, the left under King Ethelred and their right under Alfred.

The devout Ethelred decided to hold a mass before the battle, and at this moment the Danes started to advance. Alfred had to make a quick decision. Either he sent word back to Ethelred for orders, or he could give the order to advance and charge the Danish force. He made up his mind quickly. He judged that the Danes would be unbeatable once they had prepared themselves properly for battle and decided to make a pre-emptive charge while the king, his brother, was still at prayers. His own wing reacted immediately and charged

Above: View westwards along The Ridgeway towards the Saxon position.

Right: Statue of Alfred at Wantage.

with great enthusiasm, but the king's wing was slower to take up the orders. Although Alfred's men fought furiously, they were seriously outnumbered until Ethelred's wing joined in. Eventually Ethelred himself, with his personal experienced warriors, arrived to tip the balance in favour of the Saxons. King Bagsac and five of his earls were killed but King Halfden escaped.

Ethelred died soon afterwards and, in April 871, Alfred became King of Wessex. Although this was a notable victory, it was an isolated one in a string of defeats, and eventually the Saxons had to buy peace by yielding land.

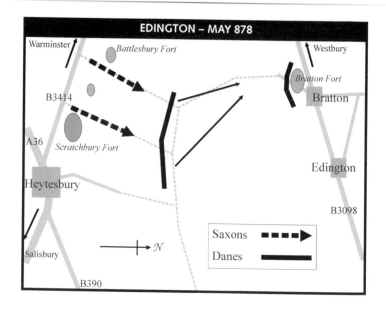

EDINGTON – MAY 878

OS: ST925475

The Danes probably dug the earthworks as their defence and Alfred attacked between the Battlesbury and Scratchbury Camps. The Danes fled towards Bratton and Edington. The Bratton White Horse was cut in the hillside to commemorate the victory. The site can be reached by a trackway leading from Heytesbury.

Alfred had succeeded to the throne of Wessex in 871, but suffered continuous reversals against the invading Danes until 878, when, having put together a large combined force, he faced them once more at Ethandun (the modern Edington, in Wiltshire). While the Danes were camped on the Downs above Edington, Alfred marched straight towards the Danes from the south past Battlesbury Camp, and then made a direct charge at them just as at Ashdown. The Danes had fortified their position by means of a ditch (the remains of which are still visible) but the charge was successful enough to make them retreat partly towards Bratton and partly towards Edington. In both cases, however, they were forced to flee again to their main camp at Chippenham some 20km to the north. The leaders of the Danes were persuaded to accept Christianity and to retire to East Anglia, forming with Northumbria and Mercia what was to become the Danelaw.

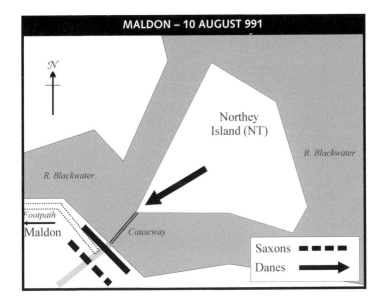

MALDON – 10 AUGUST 991

N

Northey Island (NT)

R. Blackwater

R. Blackwater

Footpath

Maldon

Causeway

Saxons ■ ■ ■ ■
Danes ➤

OS: TL868057

The battle took place on the shore opposite the causeway. This is best approached on foot from Maldon, but can also be reached from a minor road off the B1018 along a lane leading to South House Farm. This lane is not a right of way for vehicles. Northey Island is now a bird sanctuary. There is a recent statue of Brihtnoth at the water's edge in Maldon facing the Island.

The Battle of Maldon, in 991, has been captured in an epic poem, 'The Battle of Maldon'. A combined force of Danes and Norwegians had ravaged the coasts of Kent, Essex and Suffolk and sacked the town of Ipswich. It then sailed up the Blackwater river and eventually landed on Northey Island close by the town of Maldon. The local Saxons under their alderman, Brihtnoth, went to face them. The island was, and still is, connected at low tide to the mainland by a causeway, and both sides waited for the tide to fall. During this lull in activity, the Danes demanded that the English pay tribute in gold, and that on receipt of this payment the invading force would depart and leave the English in peace. Brihtnoth's reply was to challenge the Danes to fight. At first this was manifestly impossible, but as soon as the tide retreated, the Danes attempted to rush the causeway. Initially this was defended by three Englishmen, Wulfstan, Aldere and Caccus, who held at bay the raiding force, rather like Horatius on the bridge at Rome.

The Danes could make no headway until they shouted across the water asking that the English retire in order to allow the raiders

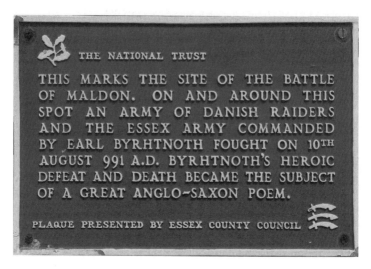

The National Trust plaque at the site of the Battle of Maldon.

to cross and give proper battle. The over-confident Brihtnoth chivalrously agreed and withdrew a short distance. Early in the battle, Brihtnoth led a body of his men into the direct fight and was wounded by a javelin. One of his officers, Wulfmaer, pulled out the javelin, but Brihtnoth was wounded yet again, this time so severely that he dropped his sword and was hacked to death. His head was cut off and his body left where it had fallen.

The English army then started to disperse, but a band of Brihtnoth's close supporters gathered round his body and fought to the death. The battle thus lasted for several hours longer than might have been expected, and the exhausted Danes made no immediate pursuit.

As a direct result of this defeat, the Saxons were forced to make the first payments to be known as Danegeld.

The body of Brihtnoth was recovered from the battlefield and buried, *sans* head, in Ely Cathedral, where it was discovered in 1769.

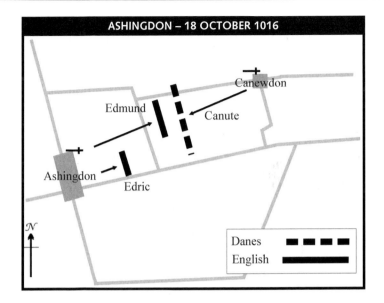

ASHINGDON – 18 OCTOBER 1016

OS: TQ883938

Edmund occupied Ashingdon Hill while Canute occupied Beacon Hill at Canewdon. Both hills now have churches. Ashingdon Church was founded by Canute to commemorate his victory. There is a monument erected at the junction just to the north of Ashingdon village.

On St George's Day, 1016, King Ethelred the Unready died leaving his son, Edmund Ironside, as his successor. Opposing him was Canute, son of Sweyn, who claimed the crown. Edmund raised an army in Mercia, and within a period of six months in 1016 fought five battles and won them all against Canute, forcing Canute to withdraw to his fastness in the Isle of Sheppey. In September 1016, Canute sailed up the Crouch and landed near Burnham to carry out yet another raid. Edmund marched against him and caught up with Canute in the area of Ashingdon, Essex, on 17 October.

While Canute occupied a defensive position on a low hill at Canewdon, Edmund was camped on Ashingdon Hill just 3km away and both armies would have been in full view of each other. Because of the closeness of his fleet, Canute had to stand and fight where he was. While he had the more seasoned fighters, Edmund had superiority of numbers.

The next morning, 18 October, Edmund divided his amy into two parts, one commanded by himself on his left, with the right wing under the command of Edric Streona, who had previously defected

A westward view from Ashingdon Church across the site of the Battle of Ashingdon, with Canewdon Church on the horizon.

to Canute but had very recently been reinstated by Edmund. Edmund charged down the hill towards the Danes and the two armies met just about halfway between the two hills. However, the right wing of Edmund's army under Edric, whether accidentally, or by treachery, failed to keep up with the rest and eventually stopped. When the armies met, Edmund's wing was outnumbered and surrounded. Edric now left the field leaving Canute with superior numbers. The outcome was in no doubt.

It is recorded that virtually the whole of the flower of the English nobility died on the field.

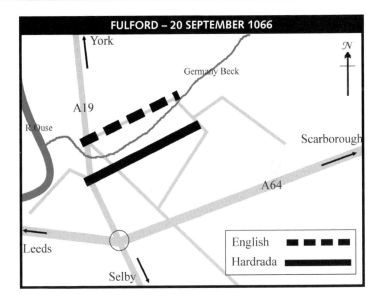

FULFORD – 20 SEPTEMBER 1066

OS: SE615495

From York take the A19 south to Fulford. The probable battlefield is 0.5km after Fulford library, where the Ouse makes a sharp bend. From the A64, take the A19 north for 1km. Authorities are scarce, but the descriptions fit the area well, with the Ouse to the west and marshes to the east.

In early September 1066, Harald Hardrada had sailed from Bergen and joined forces with Harold's brother, Tostig, Earl of Northumberland. They landed at the mouth of the Ouse, and sailed up as far as Riccal, where Hardrada disembarked and marched north with about 7,000 men. At Fulford, just south of York, were 3,000 English in a good defensive position. They were protected on their right by the River Ouse, and on their left by marshlands. At their front was Germany Beck.

Hardrada divided his army into three divisions with his least experienced men on his right wing. The early advantage was with the English as they pushed this weak right wing back, but Hardrada, reacting quickly, extended his centre towards his right wing and then used his centre forces to turn to their right and crush the English forces there. This enabled Hardrada to wheel this new right wing to the left and strike the English centre from the side. Eventually, with inferiority of numbers and without a strong defence, the English were beaten.

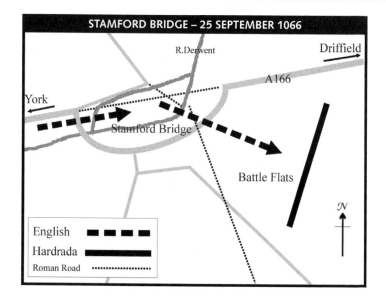

STAMFORD BRIDGE – 25 SEPTEMBER 1066

OS: SE720553

Harold approached on the Roman Road (now A166) from York, and crossed the old Roman Bridge (now dismantled) about 350m downstream from the present bridge. The battle took place on Battle Flats just south-east of the present town, where there is a monument.

After his victory at Fulford, Harald Hardrada, accompanied by Tostig, Harold Godwinson's brother, marched on York and received that city's submission. Hostages were handed over and Hardrada decamped to Stamford Bridge, some 13km east of York. In the meantime, Harold Godwinson was left in a quandary. He was expecting William of Normandy to invade in the south, but now had other invaders in the north. He decided to march north at all speed in the hope of defeating the Norwegians and then being able to return south in time to meet William.

Harold marched north at high speed, gathering troops as he went, and reached Tadcaster on 24 September. The next day he entered York, only to hear that the unsuspecting Norwegians were camped just 13km to the east. Harold gathered his tired men and immediately marched on to Stamford Bridge, catching Hardrada by surprise. The English approached from the west and to the north of the River Derwent, while the Norwegians were encamped on the south side.

Monument in the centre of Stamford Bridge commemorating the battle.

With little time to prepare a defence, Hardrada relied on a lone warrior to hold the only bridge for as long as possible. Eventually, he was overcome and Harold swept to the attack. Hardrada's army had drawn itself behind a shield wall on slightly rising ground known today as Battle Flats.

In the battle, both Hardrada and Tostig were killed. Reinforcements arrived from their base at Riccall to bolster the Norwegians, but this merely delayed the inevitable. Harold's victory was complete. It is reported that out of 300 ships that had originally carried the Norwegians to England, only twenty-four were needed to carry away the survivors.

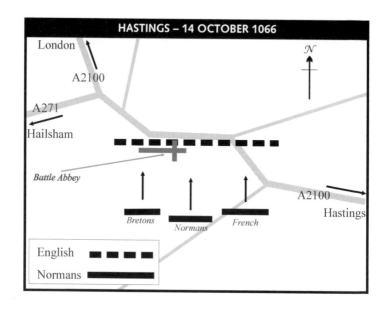

HASTINGS – 14 OCTOBER 1066

London

A2100

A271

Hailsham

Battle Abbey

Bretons   Normans   French

A2100

Hastings

English

Normans

OS: TQ747150

Battle is about eight miles (13km) north-east from the centre of Hastings. Harold's army stretched across the A2100 on a ridge. William's was in three parts attacking from the south. There is a museum and information centre in Battle which gives good information on the battle and its significance.

William, Duke of Normandy, set sail from St Valery on 28 September and landed at Pevensey with his army of some 10,000. He marched on Hastings, where he repaired the castle that Harold had dismantled

Illustration from the Bayeux Tapestry.

Battle Abbey.

earlier in the year, and settled down to wait for Harold to come to him. Harold, in the meantime, had marched at high speed from York to London following his victory at Stamford Bridge just three days earlier.

After spending some time in London to re-group, Harold set off again to meet William. William had news of the imminent arrival of Harold during the night of 13 October and marched out of Hastings at dawn the next day. During that same night, Harold's vanguard had reached what is now known as Battle. By the time that William came into sight, Harold was occupying a strong defensive position on Senlac Ridge with William about a mile away on Telham Hill.

Throughout the day, William was the attacker and Harold the defender. An initial charge by light troops of William was easily repulsed, and this prompted William to make a full-scale charge with both infantry and cavalry. This, too, was seen off, with some of William's troops retreating in the belief that William had been killed. At this retreat, some English rushed from their defensive position and were overwhelmed by William's seasoned troops.

A second cavalry charge by the Normans again failed to break the defence, but once more on the retreat of the horses, the English charged from their position and were all cut down. In the evening, an all-out attack by William's cavalry, infantry and archers broke the lines of the English. Harold was killed together with his brothers, Gurth and Leofwine, and the line of Anglo-Saxon kings had come to an end.

To celebrate his victory, William had an abbey built on the field of battle, with the altar marking the spot where Harold fell.

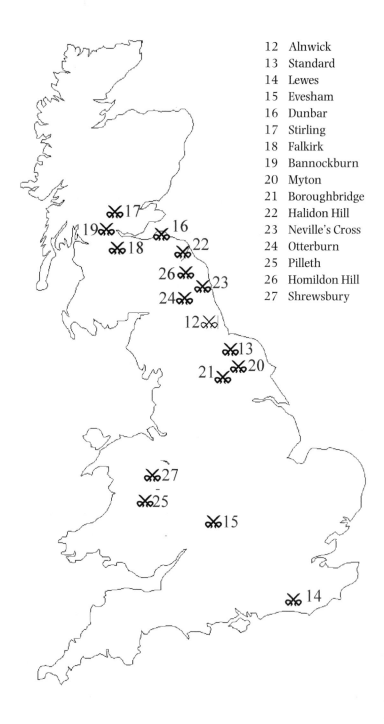

12 Alnwick
13 Standard
14 Lewes
15 Evesham
16 Dunbar
17 Stirling
18 Falkirk
19 Bannockburn
20 Myton
21 Boroughbridge
22 Halidon Hill
23 Neville's Cross
24 Otterburn
25 Pilleth
26 Homildon Hill
27 Shrewsbury

BORDERS AND BARONS

1066-1403

Williamunited what was now England in a startlingly
short time but the borders of the country with Wales
and Scotland were for many years a matter of dispute.
William's success had been achieved mainly by the strategy of
allowing his supporters to build their own castles in border areas
and to grant them wide ownership powers, on condition that
they defend the borders and keep the interior kingdom relatively
peaceful. This power, however, was double-edged, for it allowed
these new barons to act independently, and in many cases their
interests did not always coincide with those of the sovereign.

Throughout the following years, calls upon the resources of the
barons led to antagonism and even outright rebellion from time to
time. In addition to this, both Scots and Welsh saw opportunities
to invade or rebel against England while the attention of the
sovereign was occupied elsewhere, and the loyalty of the barons
could not always be relied upon by the sovereign of the day.
Indeed, some barons sided with Scots and/or Welsh whenever it
so suited their interests, and they were always trying to increase
their wealth, power and independence. For instance, the Percys
of Northumberland were strong supporters of Edward I when he
marched north to subdue the Scots in 1296, but were in league
with the Welsh and in rebellion against Henry IV at the Battle of
Shrewsbury in 1403.

Thus the period from 1066 to 1400 saw invasions of England
by Scots (Alnwick 1093, Standard 1138, Myton 1319, Neville's
Cross 1346, Otterburn 1388, Homildon Hill 1402), invasions
of Scotland by the English (Dunbar 1296, Stirling Bridge 1297,
Falkirk 1298, Bannockburn 1314, Halidon Hill 1333), rebellions
by the Welsh (Pilleth 1402), and baronial rebellions (Lewes 1264,
Evesham 1265, Boroughbridge 1322, Shrewsbury 1403). By the
end of this period, however, Scotland was no longer seen by the
English sovereign as a troublesome part of his kingdom but as an
independent country.

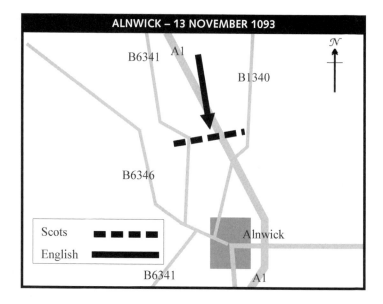

ALNWICK – 13 NOVEMBER 1093

OS: NU190147

The battlefield lies about 1km to the north of Alnwick on the B6341. There is a memorial cross on the right-hand side marking the spot where Malcolm received his mortal wound. Just to the south and west are the ruins of St Leonard's Hospital, reputedly founded on the spot where he eventually died.

In the late autumn of 1093, just twelve years after the death of William the Conqueror, King Malcolm III of Scotland crossed the border into Northumbria with a large army on yet another pillaging raid by the Scots into this still-disputed territory. By 13 November he had reached as far south as Alnwick and was camped just to the north of the town. Robert de Mowbray, the Governor of Bamburgh Castle, marched south to meet him. He faced Malcolm with a force much inferior in numbers, but surprised the large Scots army with a sudden attack. King Malcolm and his son, Edward, were killed in the fighting. A memorial cross was erected to mark the spot where the king was mortally wounded, and a hospital was founded in 1200 on the site where he eventually died.

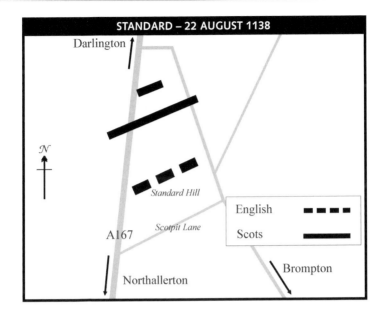

STANDARD – 22 AUGUST 1138

Darlington

N

Standard Hill

English

Scots

Scotpit Lane

A167

Brompton

Northallerton

OS: SE360977

The battlefield lies about 5km to the north of Northallerton on the A167. There is a memorial at the side of the road.

In 1138, King David I of Scotland invaded England in support of his niece, the Empress Matilda, who was disputing the English throne with her cousin, Stephen.

Stephen was heavily occupied in the south and had put the security of the north in the hands of Thurstan, Archbishop of York, who was too old to take an active part in the fighting. Instead he preached a Holy War, thus giving the English army the full weight of the Church. In York an army was raised which, although smaller than that of the Scots, marched from York to Thirsk and then to Northallerton. There it learned that the Scots were travelling south from Darlington and so it moved forward to intercept them.

About 5km north of Northallerton, on the morning of 22 August, the English army arrived at the more southerly of two hills both known as Standard Hill and its leader raised the religious standard. This consisted of a four-wheeled wagon with a large mast to which was affixed a consecrated wafer with cross-pieces and four sacred banners.

The two forces were now about 300m apart. The first charge of the Scots was made by the impetuous Galloway levies who were halted by a hail of arrows, but then Prince Henry, King David's son,

Memorial to the battle by the side of the A167.

charged against the English left and broke right through the English lines. When the English re-formed, their third line turned to attack the Scottish cavalry, who were left stranded in the rear.

All other charges by the Scots were repulsed and at one point it was thought (erroneously) that David had been killed. Eventually David admitted defeat and retreated north. The English were in no position to exploit this victory and there was no pursuit of the enemy.

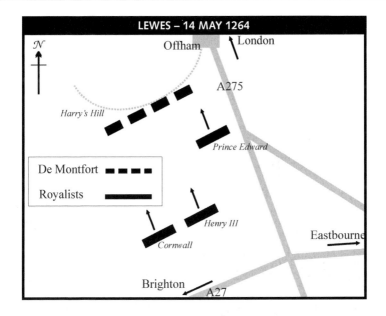

LEWES – 14 MAY 1264

OS: TQ397112

The battlefield was on the slopes of Offham Hill to the north-west of Lewes. The road leading to what was the grandstand of Lewes racecourse ran right through the middle of the battlefield on the left of the A275 just out of the town.

In 1258, the barons had forced Henry III to grant reforms giving more power to them. These became known as the Provisions of Oxford. Henry persuaded the Pope to absolve him from his oath, and King Louis IX of France annulled the Provisions. While many barons accepted the situation, some, including Simon de Montfort, refused and took up arms.

During the early part of 1264 there were battles and skirmishes between the king's forces and allies of de Montfort, and by 11 May the king had reached Lewes, where he rested in St Pancras Priory, while Prince Edward (later to be Edward I) was stationed in Lewes Castle. De Montfort had marched at speed from London to catch Henry before he gathered in any more recruits, and reached Fletching, just north of Lewes, on 13 May 1264. At dawn on the 14th, he set off towards Lewes, but at Offham took a track up to the top of the Downs. There on Harry's Hill he lined up his forces to await Henry.

The alarm was given and Prince Edward was first to react. He and his cavalry galloped out of the castle without waiting for Henry, charged up the hill towards de Montfort's forces, and swept away his

Looking north to Simon de Montfort's position on Harry's Hill.

The Seal of Henry III.

left wing. His violent pursuit took him out of contention and it was some hours before he returned.

Henry was now forced to attack up a steep hill but found de Montfort's defences and counter-attack too strong. He was forced to retreat towards the Priory south of the town. By the time Edward returned, the battle was virtually over, with de Montfort's forces rampaging through Lewes. Both Henry and Edward became prisoners of de Montfort.

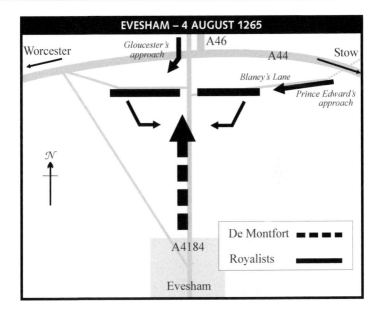

EVESHAM – 4 AUGUST 1265

OS: SP033454

The battlefield is about 2.5km north of the centre of the town on the A4184 just where it meets the A4538 leading off to the left. The A4184 is on the line of the road up which Simon de Montfort charged to try and escape the enveloping troops. There is a battle well, now sadly overgrown, to the left of the road near the junction.

Just about a year after the Battle of Lewes, Prince Edward (who was later to become Edward I) escaped from Simon de Montfort (Simon Snr) and mustered an army to recover the kingdom and rescue his father, Henry III, who was still a prisoner. Late in July 1265 he was with his army in Worcester when he had news that Simon Snr was in Hereford while de Montfort's son, Simon (Jnr) was in Kenilworth. Edward decided to attack the son first and marched directly to Kenilworth where he defeated Simon Jnr.

Upon Edward's return to Worcester, he now learned that Simon Snr had left Hereford, had crossed the Severn and had vanished. Edward reasoned that Simon Snr was probably trying to link up with his son, and accordingly set out to cut him off. He marched back towards Alcester where he sent the Earl of Gloucester on a direct line south to Evesham, while he and Roger Mortimer crossed the Avon and marched south down the eastern side. At Offenham, he re-crossed the Avon to the west and linked up with Gloucester just

Monument to the Battle of Evesham, on private land but accessible to the public.

3km north of Evesham at Green Hill. He sent Mortimer on to block the only bridge leading from Evesham by the London Road.

Simon Snr was trapped and decided that his only chance to escape was to smash through northwards at the point between Edward's two forces. However, Edward's two wings swung in onto Simon's flanks and the superior numbers of the Royalists turned the battle into a massacre. Henry III had been taken onto the battlefield as a prisoner by Simon, and, quite unrecognisable in his armour, had to shout out 'I am Henry of Winchester, your king! Do not kill me!' before being rescued.

Reconciliation between the barons and the throne came about in 1275 when the Provisions of Oxford were included in the Statute of Westminster.

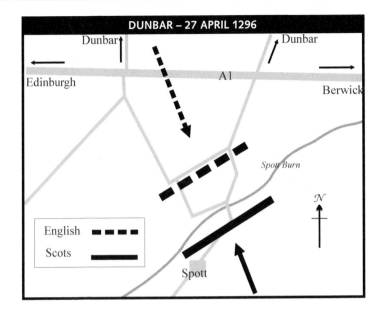

OS: NT675761
The battlefield is just to the north of the village of Spott, which is itself about two miles to the south of Dunbar. The Scots had lined up on the south bank of the Spott Burn and charged down the steep sides to attack the English as they advanced from the north.

In 1290 there was no direct heir to the Scottish throne and the Scottish succession was in turmoil. Edward I of England was asked to arbitrate and in 1292 chose John Balliol as King of Scotland with the expectation that Balliol would be nothing but a vassal king.

In 1295, the Scots rebelled and concluded a treaty with France. Edward marched north, sacked Berwick (then a Scottish town), and sent his army north to Dunbar. From Dunbar his forces turned south and met a Scottish army at Spottsmuir. A manoeuvre by the English led the Scots to think that the English were fleeing and they charged wildly. The reverse was the case and the well-organised English forces massacred the Scots. For the next ten years Scotland would be without a monarch.

Edward I.

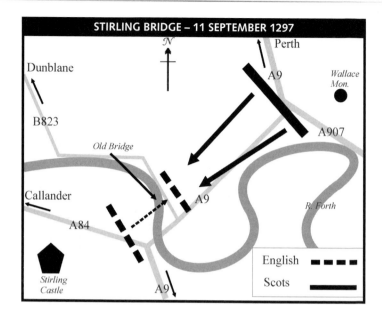

STIRLING BRIDGE – 11 SEPTEMBER 1297

OS: NS809956

The old Stirling Bridge crossed the River Forth a little way upstream from the modern bridge and its site is marked clearly on the OS map. There is now the Wallace Monument on the top of Abbey Craig from which a good view of the battle area can be obtained.

Immediately following the crushing defeat of the Scottish armies at Dunbar in 1296, Edward I put the country under the control of the Earl of Surrey as Governor and Hugh de Cressingham as Treasurer. Within a year, however, the Scots were up in arms again under the leadership of Andrew de Moray and William Wallace. The Earl of Surrey, realising that he needed to defeat the rebels, marched from Berwick to Stirling, where Wallace and Moray had taken up a position on the slopes of Abbey Craig, about one mile north-east of the bridge across the River Forth from Stirling Castle.

All attempts to negotiate with the rebels failed, and, on 11 September 1297, the English moved forward to cross the river. Some 3km upstream from the narrow bridge there was a ford capable of allowing large numbers of men to cross quickly, but Cressingham, with stubborn pride, felt that making even a small diversion like this suggested an unnecessary respect for the military prowess of the Scots.

Accordingly, the English army started to cross by the narrow wooden bridge which only allowed two men abreast to cross at a time. Wallace waited until about half the English army was across

Above: A Victorian artist's impression of the Battle of Stirling.

Right: William Wallace, Guardian of Scotland.

and then swooped down upon them. Surrey's army was cut in two and the half over the river found themselves fighting the whole of the Scottish army. The majority of those who had crossed were killed. Cressingham was among the slain and Surrey had to make a fighting retreat to Berwick. Wallace could claim a famous victory and was made sole Guardian of the kingdom of Scotland as a result.

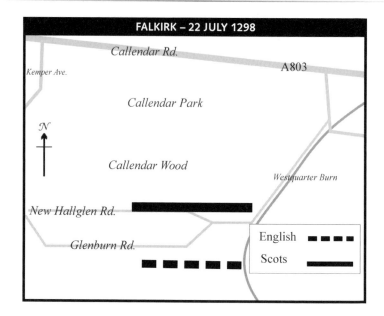

FALKIRK – 22 JULY 1298

OS: NS895785

Callendar Park lies just south of the point where the B803 leaves the A803 and where the Westquarter Burn flows in a north-easterly direction further to the south. The railway runs through the probable battle site. There is a modern cairn in Callendar Park.

The defeat at Stirling Bridge brought swift retribution from Edward I. He gathered a huge army of some 15,000 men, which included some 2,500 cavalry, and marched north to find Wallace. He caught up with Wallace near Falkirk, and found the Scots drawn up defensively with Callendar Wood to their rear, and the Westquarter Burn with marshy ground to their front. It was at this battle that the subsequently famous formation 'the schiltron' was devised by Wallace. His spearmen were drawn up in solid rings with his archers between the rings and his cavalry behind. Cavalry simply could not ride down the solid ring of spears. Edward's answer was to call upon his archers to send a hail of arrows into the spearmen. As the gaps appeared in the schiltrons, the English cavalry charged home.

Wallace, himself, escaped and fled to France.

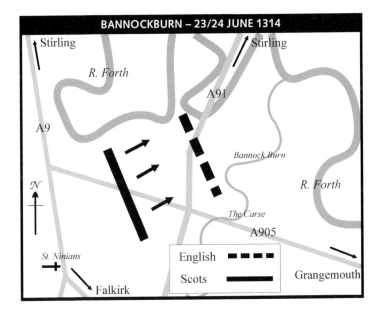

BANNOCKBURN – 23/24 JUNE 1314

OS: NS815917

The battlefield of 24 June lies in the area of low ground bounded by the A84, the River Forth and the Bannock Burn.

Robert Bruce was crowned King of Scotland on 25 March 1306 in direct opposition to the wishes of Edward I, who determined to recapture Scotland. When Edward I died early in 1307, the accession of Edward II gave Bruce the chance to take stock and consolidate. Gradually the English strongholds in Scotland were taken until by 1314 the only castle remaining in English hands was Stirling.

The governor of the castle, Sir Philip de Mowbray, made a covenant with Edward Bruce, the brother of Robert, that he would surrender the castle if it had not been relieved by 24 June 1314. Edward II could not allow the castle to fall and Robert Bruce could not allow Edward II to lift the siege. Edward II marched to Stirling and Bruce waited for him 3km south of Stirling Castle across the Stirling-Edinburgh road (now the A872). By 23 June each was ready to engage in battle.

Bruce's defences across the road were intended to dissuade Edward from using his cavalry in a charge, and the day consisted of skirmishes with no decisive breakthrough by either side. Bruce then decided to retreat from the battle, but changed his mind when Sir Alexander Seton, deserting from the English, arrived with news from the English camp. Edward had decided that he could not reach

Statue of Robert the Bruce, Scotland's national hero, who, with his succession of victories against the English, established Scotland as an independent country, recognised as such by the English Crown.

Stirling by the direct route and had given orders to march east and camp overnight next to the Bannock Burn on the Carse, an open but boggy plain. Bruce realised that the new battlefield would give him a greater advantage.

The next day, 24 June, saw the Scots now re-grouped into four schiltrons advancing towards the English. At first the English archers appeared to be winning the battle, but then the English cavalry charged the Scottish lines, obscuring the targets from the archers. The English cavalry, however, had no answer to the massed pikes and they were driven back onto their own lines. Their archers were ineffective and the infantry at the back could not get forward through the press. Eventually the English turned to escape the battle, and the schiltrons simply drove right through the English lines, with the English army now in full flight.

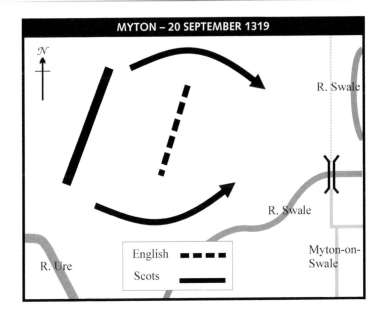

MYTON – 20 SEPTEMBER 1319

N

R. Swale

R. Swale

R. Ure

Myton-on-Swale

English ▪ ▪ ▪ ▪

Scots ▬▬▬

OS: SE428675

The battlefield is about 4.5km to the east of Boroughbridge, which is itself on the B6265, at junction 48 of the A1 (M). The battlefield today is virtually unchanged from that of 1319 other than a belt of trees across the middle and is accessed by a bridge on the same site as the original bridge.

After Bannockburn, the Scots were rampant in the north. They expelled the English from Scotland and in 1318 captured Berwick. In an attempt to recapture the town, Edward II laid siege to Berwick in 1319, but the Scots, disdaining to meet his forces head on, sent an army of some 15,000 further south into Yorkshire as marauders. They sacked Boroughbridge and were intercepted at Myton by a motley force collected by the Archbishop of York. This English army crossed the bridge at Myton (where its successor stands today) but were confused by fire and smoke from burning hay set alight by the Scots, who then surrounded the English by a pincer movement and utterly defeated them. As a direct result of this defeat, Edward had to lift the siege of Berwick and agree to a two-year truce.

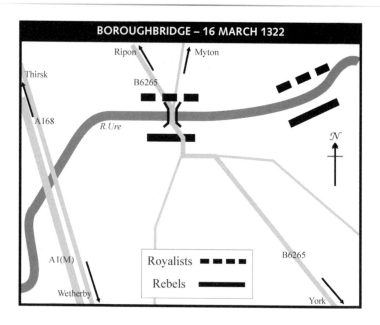

BOROUGHBRIDGE – 16 MARCH 1322

Ripon
Myton
Thirsk
B6265
A168
R. Ure
N
A1(M)
B6265
Royalists ■ ■ ■ ■
Rebels ▬
Wetherby
York

OS: SE397670

Boroughbridge is at junction 48 of the A1 (M). It is probable that the original bridge was a wooden bridge sited just upstream from the present one, and the site of the Roman ford is about 0.5km downstream.

In 1321, Edward II had taken an army to the Welsh Marches because of a rebellion by Roger Mortimer and Humphrey Bohun, Earl of Hereford. They had been expecting support from Thomas, Earl of Lancaster, but this was delayed, and they had had to concede defeat. This enabled Edward to concentrate on the north of his kingdom and he marched to Burton-on-Trent to face Lancaster.

Lancaster marched south to meet the forces of the king, but had been faced by superior forces and was forced to retreat north towards his territories in Northumberland. On 16 March 1322, now joined by the Earl of Hereford, he reached Boroughbridge on the River Ure, with the king in hot pursuit. There he found his way barred at the town by the Sir Andrew de Harcla, the Warden of Carlisle.

Harcla had drawn up his forces to guard against crossings either at the bridge or at the old Roman ford at Aldborough. The Earls of Lancaster and Hereford now decided to split their own forces with Lancaster attempting to force his way across the old Roman ford and Hereford attacking the bridge itself in the middle of the town. At the bridge, Hereford faced strong resistance, with Hereford himself

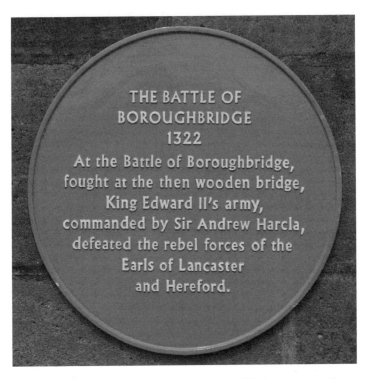

THE BATTLE OF
BOROUGHBRIDGE
1322
At the Battle of Boroughbridge,
fought at the then wooden bridge,
King Edward II's army,
commanded by Sir Andrew Harcla,
defeated the rebel forces of the
Earls of Lancaster
and Hereford.

Memorial plaque affixed to the present bridge at Boroughbridge commemorating the battle of 1322.

being killed with many of his men. The remainder retreated into the town, where they were joined by Lancaster, who had also failed in his attempt at the ford.

Lancaster agreed a brief truce with Harcla, but that night the Sheriff of York arrived from the south. In the morning, Harcla crossed the bridge to attack the rebels from the north. Lancaster was captured, imprisoned in York, and later executed. The king at last had his revenge on the leader of the barons who had murdered his favourite, Piers Gaveston, but did not live long to enjoy it. Within a few years he had been deposed and murdered.

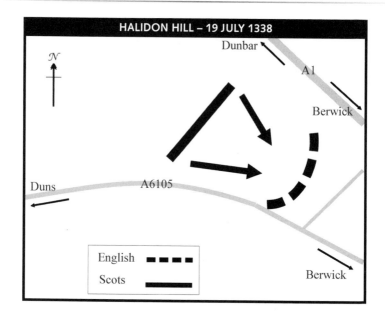

HALIDON HILL – 19 JULY 1338

Dunbar

A1

Berwick

Duns   A6105

Berwick

| English | ▪ ▪ ▪ ▪ |
| Scots | ▬▬▬▬ |

OS: NT969545

The battlefield is about 2km north-west of Berwick on the A6105. There is a lane leading off to the right with a lay-by and a noticeboard giving details of the battle. There is also a stone monument by the side of the A6105.

Edward III, in support of Edward, son of John Balliol, revoked the Treaty of Northampton and marched north to regain Berwick, which had been under Scottish rule for fifteen years. He was besieging Berwick and had obtained from its Governor an agreement that if Berwick was not relieved by 20 July it would surrender.

Archibold Douglas, the Scottish Regent, marched on Berwick with a Scots army and by 19 July was facing the English army posted on Halidon Hill some 5km north of Berwick. Because of the contract between Edward and the Governor, the onus was on the Scots to attack and this they had to do over ground of Edward's choosing. With the height of the hill for easy aiming of their longbows, and a marsh to their front, the English routed the Scots with one estimate of 10,000 dead to barely 100 on the English side.

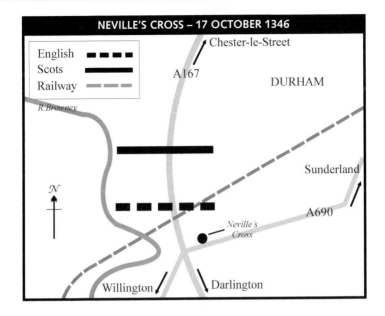

NEVILLE'S CROSS – 17 OCTOBER 1346

OS: NZ263421

The general area of the battle was astride the A167 just north of where it crosses the A690. 'Neville's Cross' is to the north of the A690 just about 100m to the east of the A167, and about 1km to the west of Durham Cathedral. The railway cuts through the battlefield.

While Edward III was destroying the French army at Crecy in August 1346 and laying siege to Calais, the French king asked the Scots king, David II, to launch a diversionary invasion. The young king responded with enthusiasm, believing that there could not be a very large force to stop him.

He marched south with perhaps as many as 20,000 troops, destroying the abbey of Lanercost on the way, and reached the outskirts of Durham on 16 October. There he rested, not realising that a substantial army had been raised to the south and was at that very moment just 12km away, at Bishop Auckland. On 17 October, the English army under, appropriately, Ralph, Lord Neville, with Henry Percy and Edward Balliol, resumed their march north, coming into sight of the Scots just before noon and taking up position on a ridge near Neville's Cross on the outskirts of Durham.

The Scots force, outnumbering the English, attacked first on their right wing, but the lie of the ground caused them to press on their own centre. This overcrowding gave the English archers a perfect

The remains of Neville's Cross which was standing when the battle was fought.

target from their superior position. While originally the Scottish left wing had the better of the fighting, the English cavalry forced it to give ground at the same time as the Scots' right wing. The Scots' left was under the command of Robert the Steward, the nephew of David, and the next in line. He soon abandoned the field, leaving David totally exposed. With the two Scottish wings in disarray and fleeing the field, the more disciplined English now surrounded the Scottish centre.

David managed to escape briefly, but was captured and imprisoned in the Tower for several years because the Scots could not raise the ransom asked for his release.

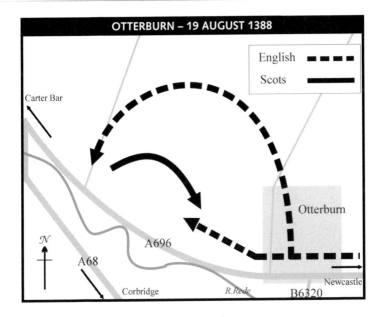

OS: NY877936

The battlefield lies about 1km north-west of the town of Otterburn on the A696. There is a cross commemorating the battle on the right-hand side of the road, together with interpretative panels depicting the course of the battle.

James, Earl of Douglas, had led a raiding army into County Durham and captured the pennant of Henry Percy ('Hotspur'), son of the Earl of Northumberland. With the honour of the Percys at stake, Hotspur followed the retreating Scots and caught up with them at Otterburn late in the day on 19 August.

He decided to send nearly half his army under Sir Thomas Umfraville on a long flanking march to attack the Scots camp in the rear. The object was two-fold – to cause confusion and to cut off any chance of retreat by the Scots. However, the majority of the Scots had, by now, left their camp and moved forward to meet the main attack, leaving their camp virtually undefended. Umfraville soon defeated the defenders, and after lingering for a while returned by the way he had come.

Meanwhile, Douglas had put into effect his own plan. This was a mirror image of Percy's except that his flanking force made a shallower circuit.

Percy had advanced along his front with his main force, forcing back the Scots with his superior numbers, but then Douglas smashed into the English right, forcing them towards the river. The running fight lasted through the hours of darkness. With their archers useless in the dark, the English were routed, and Hotspur was captured together with his brother, Ralph Percy. The flanking force returned the way it had gone to find the battle lost and virtually over.

In the main battle, Douglas was killed and a battle stone was placed on the spot where he fell by the victorious Scots.

In 1777, the Duke of Northumberland requested that a monument be erected in memory of his ancestor. The battle stone was removed and the base socket used to support the present stone, which is known as Percy's Cross.

Memorial cross by the side of the A696.

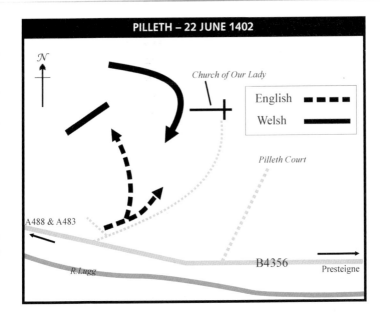

PILLETH – 22 JUNE 1402

Church of Our Lady

| English | ▪ ▪ ▪ ▪ |
| Welsh | ▬▬▬ |

Pilleth Court

A488 & A483

R.Lugg

B4356

Presteigne

OS: SO252678
The battlefield lies around the church at Pilleth on the right-hand side of the B4356 about 8km from Presteigne. There is information about the battle in the church and a holy well at the rear of the church.

A land dispute in 1400 between Owain Glyndwr (or Owen Glendower) and Lord Grey of Rutin turned into a full-scale revolt by Glyndwr when Henry IV decided in favour of Grey. For two years, Glyndwr used hit-and-run tactics in the hills of Wales against the more ponderous English armies sent out to find and defeat him. In June 1402, with a motley army of conscripts including men from Radnorshire and Herefordshire, Sir Edmund Mortimer crossed into Wales to seek out the rebels. Either he had good information of the whereabouts of Glyndwr, or Glyndwr had good information about Mortimer's intentions, for Glyndwr laid an ambush at Pilleth.

Seeing that Mortimer was marching along the road to the south of the river, Glyndwr set the church at Pilleth on fire to attract Mortimer's curiosity. Mortimer crossed the river to investigate and found himself facing a body of Welsh archers displaying the flag of Glyndwr on the hillside above the church. Upon attacking uphill this small army, he found himself in difficulties both with the slope of the hill and because his Welsh levies, seeing Glyndwr's flag, changed their allegiance and turned upon their erstwhile comrades. Glyndwr

Illustration taken from the Bayeux Tapestry showing Saxons defending their line against the Normans.

Obelisk standing just off Fernhall Lane, Waltham Abbey, marking the traditional site of Boudicca's last battle (AD 61).

View of Liddington Hill from the west. The hill is the strongest contender for 'Mons Badonicus', the site of Arthur's greatest victory (c.AD 500).

An engraved portrait of Owain Glyndwr.

himself, previously hidden behind the reverse slope of the hill, appeared unexpectedly with reinforcements to complete the rout. With his army thoroughly beaten, Mortimer surrendered and was taken prisoner.

A curious footnote is that in November that year Mortimer married Catherine, daughter of Glyndwr, and was to appear later as his ally against Henry IV. Whether this came about as a result of the failure of Henry to pay the ransom demanded, or whether the whole fight was a planned desertion, is a matter of conjecture.

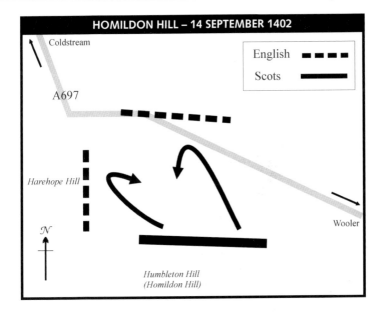

HOMILDON HILL – 14 SEPTEMBER 1402

Coldstream

A697

English

Scots

Harehope Hill

Wooler

𝒩

Humbleton Hill
(Homildon Hill)

OS: NT968294

Homildon (Humbleton) Hill lies to the south of the A697 at about 2km north-west of Wooler. The Scots were on the slopes of Humbleton Hill to the south of the road, while the English were on Harehope Hill to the west and the level ground to the north. There is a battle stone in the field to the north of the road.

In 1402 the Scots again invaded England under Archibold, Earl of Douglas, the son of James, the victor of Otterburn. Yet again they were pursued by Hotspur, and this time were caught at Homildon (now Humbleton) Hill. The Scottish army of some 10,000 men held the high ground on the lower slopes of the hill, with every confidence that they could withstand an English charge, while the English held the slopes to the west and the level ground to the north, thereby cutting the Scots off from their way to the border. Realising that the Scots' position was too strong for a frontal attack, Hotspur relied almost solely on his archers to fire volleys of arrows into the Scottish lines. The Scottish attempts to charge their way out of trouble were unsuccessful when they found the English archers could fire just as accurately while retreating. Eventually they fled the field in total disarray.

Hinton Fort, the site of the Battle of Deorham (AD 577).

Looking west towards Dunnichen Hill over the battlefield of Dunnichen Moss (AD 685) just to the east of the village of Dunnichen.

The White Horse at Bratton commemorating the Battle of Edington between Alfred and the Danes (AD 878).

Recent statue to Brihtnoth, leader of the Saxons against the Danes at Maldon.

Below: The causeway linking the island of Northey to the mainland where the Battle of Maldon was fought in AD 991.

Bottom: The church of Ashingdon, built on the site of the church originally founded by King Canute to commemorate his victory at the Battle of Ashingdon (AD 1016).

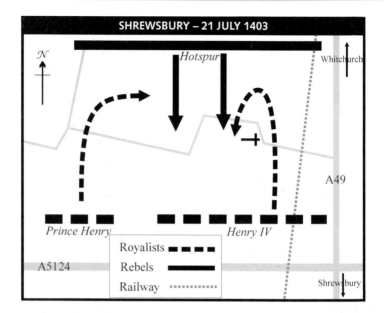

SHREWSBURY – 21 JULY 1403

OS: SJ512172

The battlefield lies around the church of St Mary Magdalene, which was built to commemorate the battle. The church is on the west of the A49 about 5km north of Shrewsbury and just north of the junction with the A53. There is a wealth of information about the battle and the contesting sides in the church.

Henry IV was in Nottingham with an army on his way north to the Borders when he heard that Henry Percy ('Harry Hotspur') had joined with Owain Glyndwr in rebellion. The reasons given were the refusal of Henry to accept part of the cost of keeping at bay the marauding Scots on the Border, and Henry's refusal to pay the ransom for the release of Sir Edmund Mortimer.

While Sir Henry Percy (the father) was raising a force in the north, Hotspur advanced towards Shrewsbury in the expectation of meeting up with Glyndwr. Prince Henry (later Henry V) was garrisoning the town and King Henry now turned south in order to join forces with him. By the time Hotspur reached Shrewsbury he discovered the town already strongly held and retreated to the north-west to Berwick. On 21 July, now realising that he had no choice but to make a fight of it, he marched east to a slight ridge and waited for the royal army.

Henry, with his son Prince Henry, marched north to meet him. Hotspur's army was deployed as one continuous line while Henry's

The church of St Mary Magdalene.

The Seal of Henry IV.

force was split into two, with Henry commanding the right and Prince Henry the left. An attempt to negotiate failed and the two armies commenced fighting with both sides using the long bow – the first time the long bow had been used by opposing forces. Originally the rebels forced back Henry, but Prince Henry on the left advanced and was able to turn and attack the rebels from the side. Hotspur was killed and the rebel army gave way. After the battle, Henry ordered a church to be built on the site to commemorate his victory.

Above: A Victorian engraving of the ruins of Battle Abbey, built by William I to commemorate his victory at Hastings (1066).

'Winner and loser' symbolised by the magnificent tomb of William the Conqueror in the Abbaye des Hommes in Caen and King Harold's insignificant-looking grave at Waltham Abbey.

The memorial cross marking the spot where King Malcolm received a mortal wound at the Battle of Alnwick (1093).

Below: 'I am Henry of Wichester, your king! Do not kill me!' – a dramatic incident enshrined on the base of the obelisk marking the Battle of Evesham (1265).

Bottom: View of the Wallace Monument on Abbey Craig from the present Stirling Bridge. The site of the Battle of Stirling (1297) is upstream from the bridge.

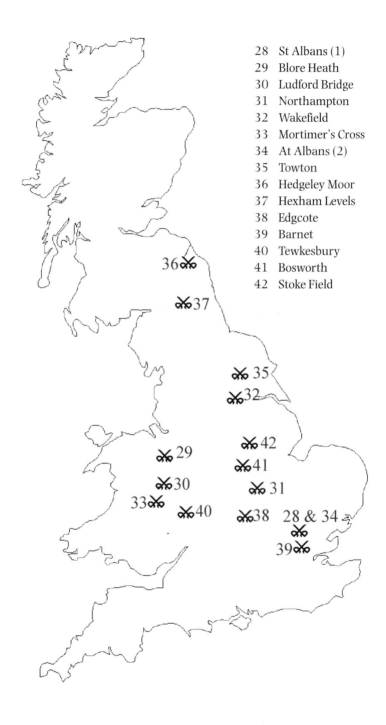

28 St Albans (1)
29 Blore Heath
30 Ludford Bridge
31 Northampton
32 Wakefield
33 Mortimer's Cross
34 At Albans (2)
35 Towton
36 Hedgeley Moor
37 Hexham Levels
38 Edgcote
39 Barnet
40 Tewkesbury
41 Bosworth
42 Stoke Field

WARS OF THE ROSES

1455-1487

O n 27 March 1454, Richard, Duke of York, became the effective Governor of England when Henry VI (son of John of Gaunt, Duke of Lancaster) suffered a mental breakdown. When Henry recovered at the beginning of 1455, he dismissed Richard and appointed Edmund, Duke of Somerset, as his chief advisor. Because of the rivalry and hatred between the Houses of York and Somerset, Richard feared for his safety and retired to his northern estates to prepare to defend himself. He then set out to march on London with the support of the Earls of Warwick and Salisbury to demand Edmund's removal. Henry, hearing this news, immediately set out to meet Richard and the two armies met at St Albans (1455). Thus began the so-called Wars of the Roses, which started as a dispute between the Dukes of York and Somerset and then developed into a struggle of power between the Houses of York and Lancaster over who should govern England.

The death of the Duke of Somerset and the victory of Richard at St Albans led to four years of a strained truce, at the end of which Henry's queen, Margaret, striving for power herself, indicted Richard and demanded the arrest of the Earl of Warwick. Civil war again loomed, but now the Yorkist forces were dispersed. Richard, himself, was at Ludlow, the Earl of Warwick in Calais and the Earl of Salisbury in Yorkshire. Henry decided to march west to Staffordshire to try and stop the Earl of Salisbury from joining Richard, but it was Henry's son Edward with Lord Audley who actually intercepted Salisbury at Blore Heath. In a bloody battle Audley was killed, and the Lancastrians defeated. Henry in the meantime continued his march and caught up with the Earl of Salisbury and Richard at Ludlow and defeated their combined forces in a bloodless battle. Richard fled to Ireland and the Earls of Warwick and Salisbury to Calais. In 1460 these latter returned to England and marched north with a very strong army. Henry, who had been campaigning in the Midlands, moved south to Northampton and waited for the Yorkists to arrive. As a result of the ensuing victory for the Yorkists, Henry became a prisoner.

Erected in 2007, this monument commemorates the Battle of Falkirk (1298) at which Wallace was defeated. It was one of the earliest battles where archers decided the outcome.

The battlefield of Myton (1319) where a marauding band of Scots utterly defeated a makeshift army organised by the Archbishop of York.

The monument at Burgh-on-Sands, Cumbria, where Edward I died in 1307 after trying, despite his illness, to lead his army to Scotland to avenge the death of John Comyn at the hands of Robert Bruce.

Following the success of his supporters at Northampton, Richard of York returned to England himself and had himself declared heir to Henry to the exclusion of Edward, Prince of Wales. Margaret now took up the king and Edward's cause with all her power and led an army later that same year against the Duke of York at Wakefield. In that battle, Richard, Duke of York, was killed, and in the aftermath, his son, Edmund, and Richard Neville, Earl of Salisbury, were captured and later executed.

Early in 1461, Edward, Earl of March, Richard of York's eldest son, who was lucky not to have been caught up in the disaster at Wakefield, gathered an army to march to London, but first had to meet and vanquish a force led by the Earls of Wiltshire and Pembroke at Mortimer's Cross. While he raced on towards London, Margaret also now turned towards London to try and rescue Henry. She was met at St Albans by the Earl of Warwick. Her victory there was complete, and she was reunited with Henry, who had been forced to accompany Warwick. Warwick escaped the field with the rump of his army and joined up with Edward at Chipping Norton. Their combined force was sufficient to persuade Margaret to retire north towards Yorkshire and Edward reached London where he was proclaimed king as Edward IV on 4 March 1461. He now determined to deal with Henry and Margaret finally and set off in pursuit with a huge force of about 36,000. Margaret and Henry's army was of like size and they met at Towton, where, after a day-long battle fought in a snowstorm, over 28,000 lay dead, and the Lancastrian cause was beyond redemption. Margaret and Henry fled north to Newcastle and Edward returned to London to be crowned king formally.

Apart from two further attempts by the Lancastrians to revive their fortunes at Hedgeley Moor and Hexham in 1464, there were now eight years of peace before new problems arose for Edward in 1469. The Earl of Warwick had been his greatest supporter but now changed sides. During 1469, 1470 and 1471 battles were fought at Edgcote, Barnet and Tewkesbury with varying fortunes, but after his victory at Tewkesbury, Edward was secure on his throne, the Earl of Warwick was dead and Henry had been executed.

The third and last phase of this series of battles started with the accession of Richard III upon Edward's death in 1483, saw two battles at Bosworth and Stoke Field, and ended with Henry Tudor (great-great-grandson of John of Gaunt, Duke of Lancaster) crowned as King Henry VII and married to Elizabeth, daughter of Edward IV, thus combining the two great Houses of York and Lancaster into the House of Tudor.

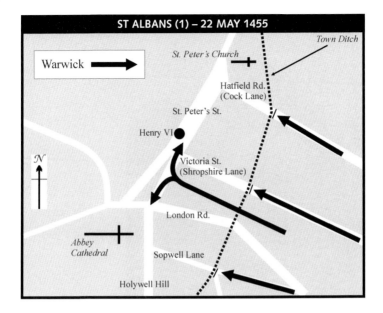

ST ALBANS (1) – 22 MAY 1455

OS: TL148072

Although the city has expanded hugely since the battle, the essential roads are still there. St Peter's Street is the same, but Holywell Street is now Holywell Hill, and Shropshire Lane is now Victoria Street. There is a plaque at the corner of St Peter's Street and Victoria Street.

Henry VI and the Duke of Somerset occupied the town centre around the market place with the Royal Standard at the south of end of St Peter's Street, while the Duke of York and the Earl of Warwick were camped just to the east outside the town ditch. As York launched his army along the two roads Sopwell Lane and Shropshire Lane (now Victoria Street) against the eastern defences, Warwick found a way to cross the ditch, by-pass the barricades and enter the market place. The point of entry was just south of Victoria Street close by the Queen's Hotel. He then wheeled to the right and left, taking the defenders by surprise. They fled from the barricades, allowing the Yorkist army to pour into the town. The outnumbered royal army was soon vanquished with the Duke of Somerset killed and the king captured. The next day, York escorted Henry back to London, swearing allegiance.

The rough stone that marks the site of the Battle of Halidon Hill (1338).

The church at Pilleth around which was fought the battle in 1402.

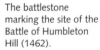

The battlestone marking the site of the Battle of Humbleton Hill (1462).

The battle church at Shrewsbury built by Henry IV to commemorate his victory (1403) at which his son Henry (later Henry V) proved his worth and Henry Percy ('Harry Hotspur') was slain.

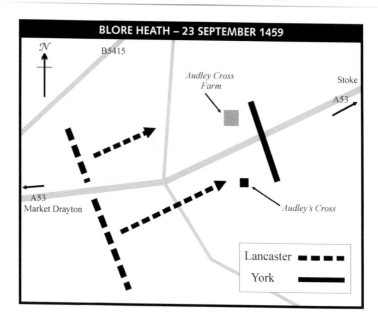

BLORE HEATH – 23 SEPTEMBER 1459

OS: SJ714352

The battlefield is about 4km east of Market Drayton on the A53 and about 1km after the junction with the B5415. Audley's Cross Farm is on the north side of the road, and Audley's Cross is on the south. The cross is in the middle of the battlefield with the armies spanning the road on both sides.

After St Albans, there followed a period of four years of a strained truce, at the end of which Queen Margaret, striving for power herself, indicted the Duke of York and demanded the arrest of the Earl of Warwick. Civil war again loomed, but the forces of the Yorkists were now dispersed. York himself was at Ludlow and the Earl of Salisbury in Yorkshire. Henry decided to march west to Staffordshire to try and stop Salisbury from joining York, but it was Lord Audley, leading the army of the young Prince of Wales, who met up with Salisbury at Blore Heath. In the ensuing bloody battle, Audley was killed. With their cavalry defeated and their leader dead, the Lancastrians broke and fled, with the Yorkists in hot pursuit, to the banks of the River Tern.

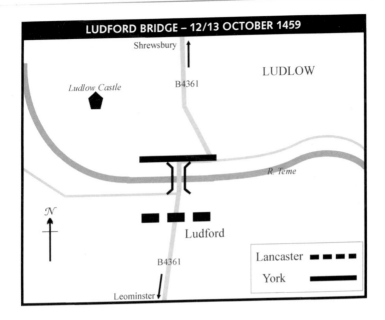

OS: SO510741

Ludford Bridge crosses the River Teme to the south of and on the outskirts of Ludlow at Ludford.

After his victory at Blore Heath, Salisbury continued to Ludlow to join Richard, Duke of York, and the Earl of Warwick. In the meantime, Henry VI was marching south with York always falling back, probably because of an ingrained reluctance to fight against troops under the king's direct command. By 12 October the two forces were facing each other across the River Teme at Ludford Bridge.

York had strong defences but inferior numbers. During the night, Andrew Trollope deserted the Yorkists and took all his men over to the king's side. This left the Yorkists in a hopeless position and much of the army fled. Next day the Lancastrians swept across the bridge and sacked the town of Ludlow and the castle. York deserted to Ireland, while Salisbury, Warwick and Edward, Earl of March, fled to Calais. The following morning the rest of the Yorkist army surrendered to Henry.

A map of England and Wales showing the extent of the conflict between the Houses of Lancaster and York in what became known as the Wars of the Roses.

Opposite ||||||||||||||||||||||||||||||||||||||||||||||||||||||||||||||||||||||||||||||||||||||||||||||||||||||||||||||||

Top left: Plaque recalling the Battle of St Albans of 1455.

Top right: Audley's Cross at Blore Heath (1459).

Centre: Ludford Bridge where the battle of 1459 was fought.

Bottom: Delapre Abbey on the site of the Battle of Northampton (1460) where Henry VI was imprisoned on the night following the battle.

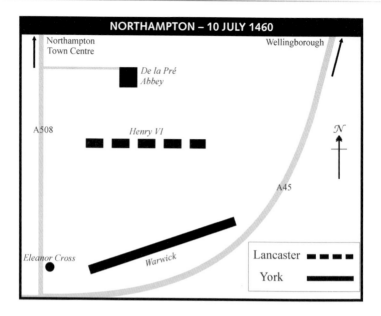

NORTHAMPTON – 10 JULY 1460

Northampton Town Centre

Wellingborough

De la Pré Abbey

A508

Henry VI

$\mathcal{N}$

A45

Eleanor Cross

Warwick

| Lancaster | ▪ ▪ ▪ ▪ |
| York | ▬▬▬ |

OS: SP764592

The major part of the battlefield remains open as the parkland of Delapre Abbey about 2km south of the city centre. This lies to the east of the A508 immediately south of the River Nene and is now substantially a golf course. Good views over the area can be obtained from the abbey gardens.

Salisbury, Warwick and the Earl of March returned to England in 1460, took Sandwich, and established a base there. By July they had amassed a very strong army and taken London. Salisbury was left in London to subdue the Lancastrian forces in the Tower of London, while Warwick and March moved northwards. Henry VI, who had been campaigning in the Midlands, moved south to Northampton and waited for the Yorkists to arrive.

Although the Yorkists outnumbered the Lancastrians, the sides were effectively evenly matched because of the bad weather and the strong defensive position now adopted by Henry, and the fighting was inconclusive until, as at Ludford, treachery of a leader decided the outcome. Here it was Lord Grey on the king's side who changed sides and let in the Yorkists. Many of the Lancastrian leaders were killed and Henry became a prisoner yet again.

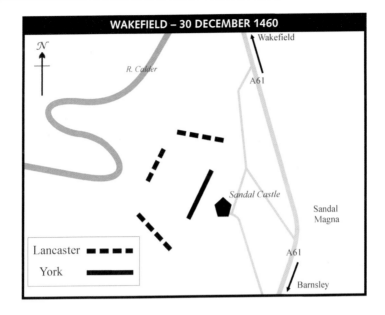

WAKEFIELD – 30 DECEMBER 1460

Lancaster ■ ■ ■ ■
York ▬▬▬

OS: SE335182

The ruins of Sandal Castle lie just to the west of the A61 Barnsley to Wakefield road and about 3km south of Wakefield. It is well signposted, and the battle took place in the grounds to the north between the castle and the River Calder. There is a monument to the Duke of York who fell in the battle.

After Northampton, Richard, Duke of York, now returned to England and was declared heir to Henry VI to the exclusion of Edward, Prince of Wales. This was not to the liking of Queen Margaret who summoned all the king's supporters, including the Duke of Somerset, to join her in the north. This threat had to be met by the Duke of York and Richard Neville, Earl of Salisbury, who left London in the middle of December and arrived at Sandal Castle, Wakefield, while the Lancastrian force gathered at Pontefract.

The Lancastrians had superiority in numbers, but did not have the siege engines to capture Sandal Castle. They therefore suggested a truce until after Epiphany, to which York agreed. The Lancastrian leaders realised that as time passed, more supporters of York would arrive, and they devised several stratagems to draw York from his defences. One involved inserting several of their own supporters into the castle in the guise of Yorkist reinforcements.

The truce was still officially running on 30 December when York was induced to leave the safety of the castle. Whatever the

Ruins of Sandal Castle which was occupied by the Yorkists during the Battle of Wakefield (1460).

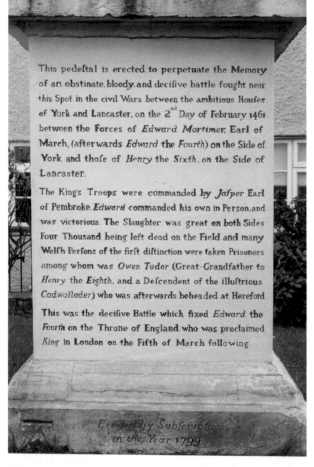

This pedeſtal is erected to perpetuate the Memory of an obstinate, bloody, and deciſive battle fought near this Spot in the civil Wars between the ambitious Houſes of York and Lancaster, on the 2nd Day of February 1461 between the Forces of *Edward Mortimer*, Earl of March, (afterwards *Edward* the *Fourth*) on the Side of York and thoſe of *Henry* the *Sixth*, on the Side of Lancaster.

The King's Troops were commanded by *Jaſper* Earl of Pembroke. *Edward* commanded his own in Person, and was victorious. The Slaughter was great on both Sides Four Thousand being left dead on the Field and many Welſh Perſons of the firſt diſtinction were taken Priſoners among whom was *Owen Tudor* (Great-Grandfather to *Henry* the *Eighth*, and a Deſcendent of the illuſtrious *Cadwallader*) who was afterwards beheaded at Hereford

This was the deciſive Battle which fixed *Edward* the *Fourth* on the Throne of England who was proclaimed *King* in London on the Fifth of March following.

Erected by Subſcription in the Year 1799

This unique monument was erected in 1799 to 'perpetuate the memory' of the battle known as Mortimer's Cross (1461).

Percy's Cross, close by the east side of the A697 immediately south of the Hedgeley Moor battlefield (1464).

Monument to the Battle of Barnet (1471) at the junction of the A1000 and the A1081.

The battlefield of Edgecote (1469).

The monument in memory of the Duke of York.

cause the Lancastrians under Somerset now fell upon the Yorkist forces. York was killed in the ensuing battle, while his younger son, Edmund, Earl of Rutland, was killed on Wakefield Bridge and the Earl of Salisbury was captured, taken to Pontefract and executed the next day.

Opposite: The burial site of the Battle of Mortimer's Cross.

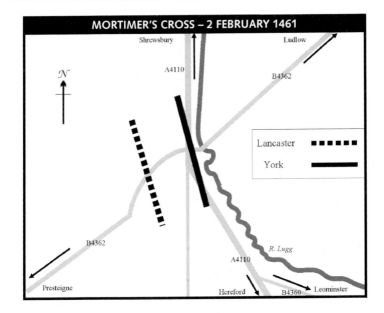

MORTIMER'S CROSS – 2 FEBRUARY 1461

Shrewsbury   Ludlow

A4110

B4362

$\mathcal{N}$

Lancaster ■ ■ ■ ■ ■ ■

York ▬▬▬▬▬

B4362

R. Lugg

A4110

Presteigne   Hereford   B4360   Leominster

OS: SO430626

Mortimer's Cross is about 25km north of Hereford on the A4110 at the junction of the B4362. The Yorkists were deployed across the B4362 blocking the way of the Lancastrians from Wales. There is a monument at Kingsland about 2km to the south and just off the A4110.

Following the disaster of Wakefield, Edward, Earl of March, York's eldest son, and soon to be Edward IV, gathered an army to advance against Queen Margaret, but first had to meet a Lancastrian force led by the Earls of Wiltshire and Pembroke, which had landed in Wales. The two armies met at Mortimer's Cross. The Yorkists outnumbered the Lancastrians and the battle was decided when the Lancastrian centre collapsed. Among the casualties on the Lancastrian side was Owen Tudor, second husband of Catherine, the widow of Henry V, father of Edmund, Earl of Pembroke and grandfather of Henry VII.

Heraldic emblem displayed on the wall of the battle information centre at Bosworth (1485).

Bloody Meadow, where some of the fiercest fighting took place at the Battle of Tewkesbury (1471).

The battlefields of (top) Stoke Field (1487), (centre) Solway Moss (1542) and (bottom) Ancrum Moor (1545).

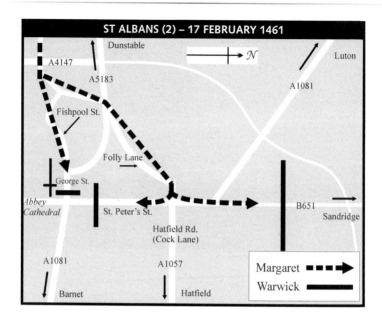

OS: TL154083

See first Battle of St Albans. This battle also spread to the north into Barnard's Heath and even the village of Sandridge. Barnard's Heath is now wholly overbuilt, but the early earthworks of Beech Bottom can still be seen.

Following the Lancastrian victory at Wakefield, Queen Margaret turned towards London to try and rescue the king. In order to meet this threat, Richard Neville, Earl of Warwick, led his army out of London and marched to St Albans. Warwick spread his army along the line of Beech Bottom to Sandridge in order to meet any advance from Wheathampstead or Luton and left a small post in the centre of the town.

However, the queen led her force down Watling Street from Dunstable during the night, crossed the River Ver and attacked from the west at dawn. The first attempt was by George Street but that was held up by the Yorkist archers. Sir Andrew Trollope then made a second attack to the north-west of the town, entered St Peter's Street from the north, and by noon the town was in Lancastrian hands.

Above: The site of the barricade in George Street.

Opposite: An engraved portrait of Henry VI.

The time taken to capture the town allowed the Yorkists to re-organise. A forward detachment re-grouped just to the north with formidable defences, with Warwick himself, further north, still trying to re-align his main force. The Lancastrians launched a third attack and once again treachery had a hand to play in that a Captain Lovelace deserted the Yorkists in favour of the queen, tipping the scales in favour of the Lancastrians. By the time that Warwick had managed to get his men into position, his forward troops on Barnard's Heath had broken and were streaming away. Once again the Lancastrians moved up to the attack.

A fourth battle at Sandridge raged until dusk when Warwick, with some 4,000 remaining men, managed to leave the field and join up with Edward, Earl of March, at Chipping Norton. Henry VI, who had been brought to the battle as a prisoner of Warwick, was restored to his queen and son.

Top: Powick Bridge (1642).

Above: View of the battlefield of Edgehill (1642).

Left: A colourful marker at the site of the Battle of Lansdown (1643).

Opposite: ||||||||||||||||||||||||||||||||||||||||||||||||||||

Top: Edgcote House where Charles I stayed overnight on the eve of the Battle of Edgehill (1642).

Centre: A view over the battlefield of Braddock Down (1643).

Bottom left and right: Monuments to the Battles of Hopton Heath (1643) and Stratton (1643).

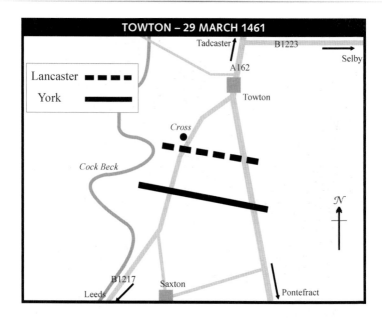

TOWTON – 29 MARCH 1461

OS: SE478386

The battle took place just south of Towton, which is itself some 2km south of Tadcaster on the A162. Immediately to the south of Towton the B1217 branches to the right. Just over 1km on the B1217 by the right side of the road is the cross erected to commemorate the death of Lord Dacre.

After his victory at Mortimer's Cross, Edward, Earl of March, raced to London and had himself proclaimed King Edward IV, while Margaret, victor at St Albans, retired north towards York. Edward now turned his sights towards Margaret and marched to Pontefract, where he joined Richard Neville, Earl of Warwick, and William, Lord Fauconbridge, and their forces. The forces of Margaret and Henry VI, under the leadership of the Duke of Somerset with the Earl of Northumberland and Lord Dacre, took up a defensive position just south of Towton to await the coming of Edward.

The day-long battle commenced at dawn on Palm Sunday in a snow-storm with a strong wind in the faces of the Lancastrians. Fauconbridge ordered his archers to fire one arrow each into the enemy line and then smartly retire. The Lancastrian archers replied as expected with volley after volley of arrows, all of which fell short. When the barrage ceased, the Yorkist archers went forward and gathered up most of the arrows, leaving some as a barricade against any Lancastrian advance.

The Towton monument by the side of the B1217.

This soon came and was met by a storm of arrows, which were now plentiful on the Yorkist side. At first things went well with the Lancastrians, but gradually the Yorkist forces gained control as their re-inforcements arrived on their right. This enabled them to out-flank the Lancastrians with the result that the morale of the Lancastrians collapsed and the army retreated in disarray towards the river. The encounter lasted some ten hours with some 28,000 killed.

Margaret and Henry VI fled north to Newcastle, and Edward returned to London to be formally crowned king.

Left: The monument to John Hampden who fell at the Battle of Chalgrove (1643).

Centre left and right: Memorials to the Battles of Adwalton Moor (1643) and Winceby (1643).

Bottom: The church at Acton (Battle of Nantwich).

Top left: Memorial for the Battle of Cheriton (1644).

Top right: Monument on the battlefield of Marston Moor (1644).

Above: Now a school, Shaw House was used by Charles I as his headquarters during the second Battle of Newbury (1644).

Right: The obelisk at Naseby (1645).

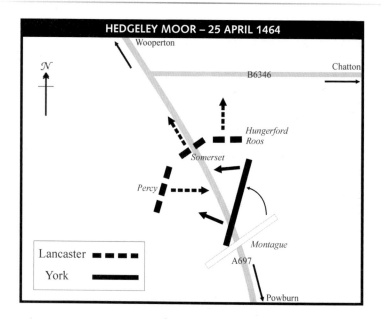

HEDGELEY MOOR – 25 APRIL 1464

OS: NU049197

Hedgeley Moor is about 15km north-west of Alnwick on the A697, just south of the junction with the B6346. There is an informative panel at the roadside in a clump of trees at the spot where Sir Ralph Percy is said to have charged the Yorkist line, and there is a weathered cross, 'Percy's Cross', just off the road on the way to Anwick.

Three years after the destruction of the Lancastrian army at Towton, an attempt was made to resuscitate their fortunes in Northumberland. A Lancastrian force with Somerset (who had previously supported Edward IV, but had now declared for Henry VI), Roos, Hungerford and Sir Ralph Percy met a Yorkist force under John Neville, Marquess of Montagu, at Hedgeley Moor in April 1464. Roos and Hungerford with their men drew off, but Sir Ralph stayed and lost the battle and his life. Tradition has it that Percy's horse made a giant leap during his last charge. Stones have been erected at 'Percy's Leap' to illustrate this feat.

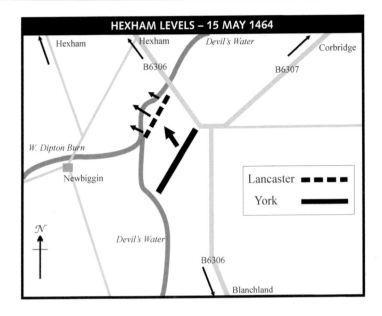

HEXHAM LEVELS – 15 MAY 1464

OS: NY958614

The battlefield is at Hexham Levels to the south of Hexham at the junction of the B6306 and the B6307. The fighting took place to the west of the junction in the meadows that slope down to the river (Devil's Water).

This, the last battle of the first phase of the Wars of the Roses, was more a rout than a battle. With the intention of challenging Henry VI, who was still in Northumberland, Montagu left Newcastle travelling east towards Hexham. To the south of Hexham, he came across Somerset, his opponent at Hedgeley Moor, early in the morning. He lined up his forces quickly and immediately charged down the slope to where the Lancastrian army was lined up on the banks of the Devil's Water. Some of the Lancastrians fled at the sight of the Yorkists, leaving their comrades heavily outnumbered. The battle can not have lasted long for Somerset was summarily executed in Hexham that same day. Many other prominent Lancastrians were executed in the days following.

King Charles' Tower at Chester.

Charles II fled from this house after his defeat at the Battle of Worcester (1651).

The Boath Dovecote at Auldearn where there is an information centre on the battle.

The Gordon Stone, a memorial to Lord Gordon who died in the Battle of Alford (1645).

Glen Shiel.

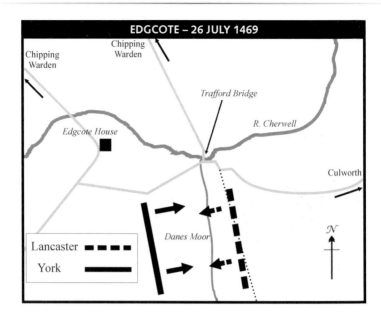

EDGCOTE – 26 JULY 1469

OS: SP519467

The site of the battle is on Danes Moor about 3km to the south-east of Chipping Warden and just 1.5km due south of Trafford Bridge. The road running north/south at the bridge is still called Welsh Road, and the stream, either side of which the armies lined up, joins the River Cherwell at this point.

Five years after Hexham, with Henry VI captured and in the Tower of London, there appeared to be no challenge to Edward IV, but now there were disputes between Edward and Warwick, with the latter deciding to resort to arms. This led to a revival of Lancastrian activity and a rebel army marched south to link up with Warwick who had taken London. The rebels intercepted a Welsh force under the command of the Earl of Pembroke which was marching east to join Edward IV at Nottingham. The armies met at Edgcote, and with Pembroke heavily outnumbered the outcome could only be delayed. Eventually his army was defeated and he was captured. As was now becoming the custom, he was executed the next day.

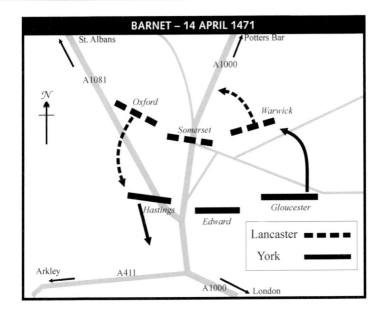

BARNET – 14 APRIL 1471

OS: TQ247079

Barnet is on the A1000 on the northern outskirts of London, about 4km to the south-east of junction 23 on the M25. The centre of the battlefield is to the north of the junction of the A1000 with the A1081. At the junction with Kitts End Road there is a monument.

In 1470, with the Earl of Warwick now supporting Henry VI, Edward IV and his younger brother Richard of Gloucester sailed to France seeking refuge in Burgundy, thus leaving power in the hands of Warwick and Henry VI. However, in March 1471, while Warwick was in the north, Edward crossed back into England. He landed in the north and marched south towards Coventry where the Earl of Warwick was based. Warwick declined battle, Edward continued to march south, was accepted in London, and took Henry prisoner. Warwick in turn marched south, and by dusk on 13 April the two armies met at Barnet.

Each army was arrayed in three 'battles', but because Edward had arrived in the dark, he misjudged the exact line-up of Warwick's forces, and each of the two right wings overlapped the opposite left wing. On the morning of 14 April, in a thick fog, the two sides advanced. Warwick's right wing, under the Earl of Oxford, drove back the Yorkist left all the way into Barnet and through the town. Eventually he gathered in some of his forces and led them back up the hill towards the battle.

Above: The Glenfinnon Monument.

Left: The memorial cairn at Culloden (1746).

Opposite ||||||||||||||||||||||||||||||||||||||||||||

Top and bottom: This rugged monument recalls the last clan battle recorded in Scotland at Roybridge. The Mackintoshs claimed ownership of land occupied by the MacDonells living in Keppoch. When the Mackintoshs marched on the village to realise their claim the MacDonells fled up their hill at Maol Ruadh (Mulroy). Once the Mackintoshs relaxed, flushed with their success, the MacDonells charged down the hill to attack them. (OS: NN271815)

THE BATTLE OF MULROY
4th August 1688

On the hill opposite,
the MacDonells of Keppoch
defeated the Mackintoshs
in the last inter—clan
battle fought in Scotland.

A Victorian engraving of the Battle of Barnet.

In the meantime, pressure from the Yorkist right had achieved something similar but with greater discipline, and the two armies had wheeled in an anticlockwise direction. Thus Warwick's centre, instead of facing due south, was now facing south-east, and some of his men now fired upon the returning Oxford men, mistaking them for enemy reinforcements. The cry of 'Treason' rang out from Oxford's men and caused confusion in the ranks of the Lancastrians. These, believing Oxford's men to have deserted to the enemy, now fought them furiously, and the Lancastrian battle formation quickly degenerated into chaos. Edward now brought up his reserves, pressed home his advantage in the ensuing melee and the battle was won. Warwick was killed on the field.

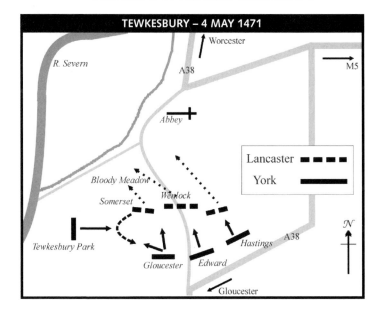

TEWKESBURY – 4 MAY 1471

OS: SO890318

Tewkesbury is at junction 9 of the M5. The battlefield is south of the town astride the A38 where it leaves the by-pass and heads straight into the town centre. The turning to Tewkesbury Park leads south to Bloody Meadow. There is a monument in the Vineyards, a park to the south of the abbey.

On the very same day that Edward IV was winning the Battle of Barnet, Queen Margaret, with her son, Prince Edward, landed at Weymouth to claim back the throne. Her immediate priority was to cross over into Wales at the first opportunity to join up with her supporters, and that meant reaching the bridges at Gloucester, or, failing that, at Tewkesbury. She was barred from entering Gloucester and was forced to march on to Tewkesbury. Edward, marching from London, intended to cut her off, but missed her just north of Bristol. He then took a direct line to Tewkesbury and followed her. By the evening of 3 May, both armies were in battle formation.

The queen put Edmund, Duke of Somerset, in overall charge and he also commanded the right wing. In her centre was Lord Wenlock, who had fought for Lancaster at St Albans, then for York at Towton, and now again for Lancaster. For Edward there was Richard, Duke of Gloucester (to be Richard III) on his left, while Edward himself commanded the centre.

A monument to the battle with Tewkesbury Abbey in the background.

The Duke of Somerset made the first move. He tried an outflanking movement to Gloucester's left, but was himself outflanked and came under fire from two sides. His force was gradually driven back into Bloody Meadow, where they were cut down. Somerset managed to withdraw to the main lines, only to find that Wenlock had remained in his place and had not moved to give him support when he sorely needed it. Somerset accused Wenlock of being a traitor, drew his battleaxe and slew him on the spot in rage. With no leader, the centre inevitably crumbled and the battle was lost.

During the fighting Prince Edward, Margaret's son, was killed. Somerset was caught and executed two days after the battle. Henry VI, for so long a prisoner, was executed in the Tower of London, and Margaret captured. She, however, was ransomed by the King of France.

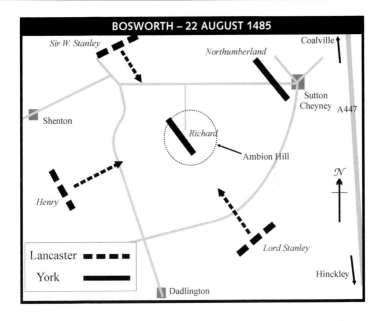

BOSWORTH – 22 AUGUST 1485

OS: SK400001

The Bosworth Interpretation Centre is on Ambien Hill which is easily reached from Sutton Cheyney, itself 2km west of the A447 and 5km north of Hinckley. Richard had reached Ambien Hill from Sutton Cheyney, and Henry was camped at White Moors about 5km away to the south-west.

Richard III (of York) met Henry Tudor (of Lancaster) at Bosworth on 22 August 1485. Richard's army, together with those of Lord Stanley and Sir William Stanley, outnumbered Henry. Richard had encamped on Ambien Hill facing south-west towards Henry's forces, with Lord Stanley's army to his south, and Sir William's forces to the north. At his rear was the Earl of Northumberland with a reserve of some 2,000 men.

The day commenced with a forward movement by Henry's troops towards Ambien Hill. As they approached, they came up against the marshy ground at the foot of the hill and had to change direction, following roughly the course of the railway. When they reached what is now Shenton station, they re-formed in order to attack Richard up the hill.

Richard's forces moved down to meet them and battle commenced with the Stanleys also advancing. However, when the Stanley forces began attacking his own forces, Richard realised that both Stanleys had changed their allegiances yet again. He must have looked

Ambien Hill with Richard III's standard flying.

hopefully to his rear expecting Northumberland to move up with his reserves, but when Northumberland remained in his place at the rear and declined to come up in support, he realised that he was going to lose the day. Richard was nothing if not a good and brave soldier; he had proved it again and again in previous battles. Now, either in rage or in despair, he charged down the hill into the thick of the fighting but became bogged down in the marsh and was killed. As only once before at Hastings, a reigning king had been killed on a battlefield in England and all fighting ceased.

After the battle, Henry's forces, together with the traitors, the Stanleys, collected on what is now Crown Hill, some 3km south of Ambien Hill. There, Lord Stanley placed Richard's battered crown on Henry's head and hailed him as Henry VII.

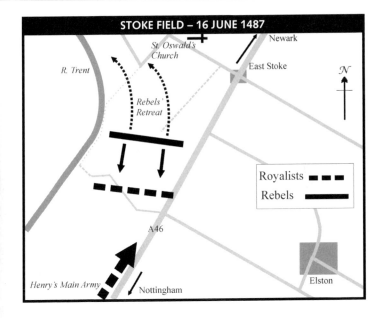

STOKE FIELD – 16 JUNE 1487

OS: SK744496

The village of East Stoke is on the A46, 5km south-west of Newark.
From the village crossroads, Church Lane leads west towards Stoke
Hall and St Oswald's Church. The first turning on the left, Humber
Lane, leads to the heart of the Yorkist lines. There is information on
the battle in St Oswald's Church.

Two years after Bosworth, a rebellious army of Yorkists led by the
Earl of Lincoln crossed from Ireland, declaring Lambert Simnel to
be 'Edward VI'. Landing in Lancashire, they marched across the
Pennines into Yorkshire and then south into Nottinghamshire. At
East Stoke, just south of Newark, they were intercepted by Henry VII.
The rebels had drawn up on a line almost east-west on a slight ridge
and attacked Henry's army as soon as its vanguard came into sight
from the south. At first things went the way of the rebels, but as the
royalist reinforcements joined in the fighting the rebels were driven
back over the ridge towards the River Trent. Red Gutter is so named
because of the slaughter that took place.

43 Flodden
44 Solway Moss
45 Ancrum Moor
46 Pinkie

THE TUDOR WARS

1513-1547

When in 1513 Henry VIII invaded France, Louis XII of France asked James IV of Scotland for help. The help given was to invade England with an army of some 40,000. After harassing the northern counties, and with his numbers falling, James decided to make his way back to the border. The English, with an army of some 25,000 gave chase and caught up with the Scots at Flodden in September 1513. In the ensuing battle, the Scots lost their king, twelve earls, fourteen lords and some 10,000 fighting men.

In 1542 the Scots were back in England again, this time under James V, and were defeated at Solway Moss. When James V died a month later leaving a week-old daughter, Mary, as Queen of the Scots, Henry decided that a marriage to his own son, the infant Edward, Prince of Wales, would bring the Scots within the power of his rule. Originally, the Scots accepted the plan, but later the marriage treaty was repudiated, leading to raids by the English into the Borders. However, in 1545 victory at the Battle of Ancrum Moor gave some respite to the Scots until Henry died in 1547.

The Duke of Somerset, as Protector of the Realm, was still determined to force the marriage between Mary and Henry's son, Edward VI, on a reluctant Scotland. This led to an invasion by the English in September 1547 with the English army, supported by its fleet, meeting a larger Scottish force at Pinkie, just east of Edinburgh. Once again the losses on the Scots side were heavy, but although the battle was won by Somerset, his ultimate aim was not achieved. By 1548, Mary was in France about to marry the Dauphin.

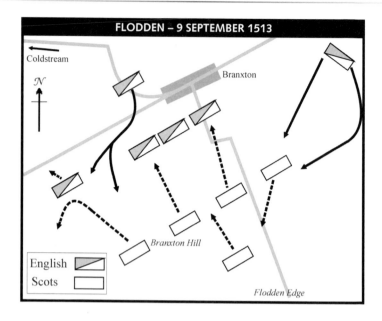

FLODDEN – 9 SEPTEMBER 1513

Coldstream

Branxton

N

Branxton Hill

English

Scots

Flodden Edge

OS: NT889373

Branxton village is about 20km south-west of Berwick-upon-Tweed via the A698 and then the A697 in the direction of Wooler. Leaving the church on the right, the battlefield is marked and the way leads to the monument on Piper's Hill. The Scots on Branxton Hill were south-east from the monument.

When in May 1513 the young Henry VIII took an army of 25,000 to France, Louis XII of France invoked a treaty with Scotland and called for James IV to bring Scotland into the struggle with England. James, ignoring the historical precedents of such an action, did not hesitate and drafted together a large force amounting to 40,000 to 50,000 men. He declared war on 11 August and invaded England at Coldstream on 22 August. In short order he reduced the castles of Norham, Etal and Ford, and at the latter he waited for the English response.

Thomas Howard, Earl of Surrey, had been charged with the defence of the north in Henry's absence, and he had set about vigorously to gather an army together and make for the north. He reached Alnwick on 3 September with a force of 26,000. He sent a message to James challenging the Scots to do battle by 9 September at the latest. To this James agreed and took up a strong defensive position astride the road from Alnwick along Flodden Edge. On seeing the strength of the

The monument on Piper's Hill.

Scots position, Surrey decided on a long flanking movement to the east, so as to come round behind the Scots position.

The Scots now abandoned their defences on Flodden Edge, turned round and took up a new defensive line on Branxton Hill facing north-west, while the English army formed up on a ridge running from Piper's Hill in the west to Mardon in the east (with a further column still marching towards the battlefield) and facing south-east.

The battle started when the Scots left wing charged and overran the English right. Two things happened as an immediate result. The reserve cavalry of the English swept to their right and rolled up the Scottish left wing, and the Scottish centre followed up by charging towards the English line, which held steadfastly. In the meantime the fourth English column had advanced circumspectly on the east, and this column now swept upon the unsuspecting Scots from the side. Having driven off the Scots right wing, this column now attacked the Scots centre from the rear and at the same time the English cavalry turned east and attacked the same Scots centre from its side. Victory was crushing and James IV was killed in the action.

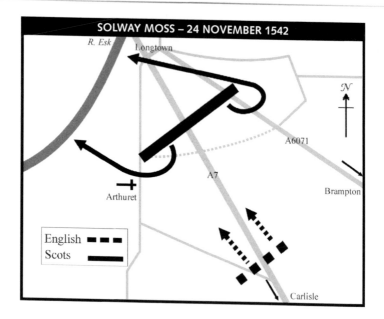

OS: NY381675

The battlefield lies between Longtown, on the A7, and St Michael's Church, Arthuret. The church can be reached by taking the road opposite the A6071 at the crossroads in the middle of Longtown and is about 3km out of the town. The Scots had crossed the River Esk at the site of the existing bridge.

In October 1542 an English raiding party had burnt Roxburgh and Kelso. James V of Scotland retaliated by sending an army of some 17,000 to raid the country north of Carlisle. The local English commander raised a small force of 3,000 to try and stop them and the two forces met just south of what is now Longtown. When the Scots saw the pennants of the English on the hilltop, they assumed that there was a much larger force following up, and initially started to march towards them, but without much in the way of fighting, they soon turned and retreated towards the Esk, harried by the English cavalry. Although some of the Scots took part in a spirited rearguard defence, many Scots were taken prisoner and many more fled. It is said that as result of the shame felt by James he died within a month of the battle.

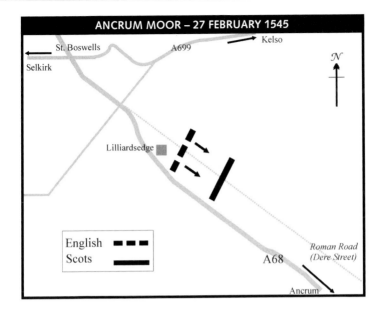

ANCRUM MOOR – 27 FEBRUARY 1545

English ■ ■ ■
Scots ▬▬▬

OS: NT619272
The battle took place astride the present A68 about 4km north-west
of Ancrum. The two armies had marched and met each other along
the Roman road (Dere Street), the line of which runs to the east of
the present A68. There is a monument on the summit of the ridge
where the battle was fought.

Henry VIII planned to betroth his son, Edward, to the infant Mary,
Queen of Scots, but this was not to the liking of the Scots politicians.
Henry therefore decided to teach them a hard lesson. He sent a
foraging army to lay waste southern Scotland. The Earl of Angus,
previously friendly towards the English, now took up arms against
them and led a small army to seek the marauding band. The English
had burned Melrose and were marching south with their booty,
when they were seen by the Scots at Ancrum Moor. The Scots drew
up in formation behind the crest of a ridge, which hid them from the
enemy and led their horses to a rise in their rear. When the English
marched forward hastily, thinking that the Scots were withdrawing,
they were caught unawares. In their confusion, the Scots charged
home and gained a complete victory and revenge.

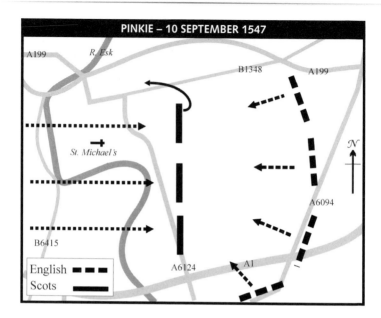

PINKIE – 10 SEPTEMBER 1547

OS: NT361716

The main battle was fought in the area bounded by the A1, the A6124, the A6094 and the B1348. St Michael's Church can be reached by Church Lane off Inveresk Road, or by Inveresk Gate off Inveresk Brae.

Henry VIII had died in January 1547, leaving a nine-year-old sickly boy, Edward VI, on the throne. The Duke of Somerset was determined to marry the boy to the infant Mary, Queen of Scots, and sent an army north to enforce this decision. It met a larger Scottish force on the banks of the River Esk about 10km east of Edinburgh at Pinkie.

Pinkie is the first battle of Britain where a land army was supported by a naval bombardment. The Scots were in a strong defensive position on the west bank of the Esk, with no weak points. The English had a much more extended position to the east on the slopes of Carberry Hill and Falside Hill, and their fleet was just off the coast offering cannon fire into the flank of the Scots.

On 9 September, a reckless cavalry charge by the Scots over the river to the east side was met by the English cavalry and this arm of the Scots army was utterly destroyed. An offer by the Earl of Arran either to give the English safe conduct home or personal combat was rejected, and battle commenced next day in the morning.

The English gradually advanced from the east in four columns with a further cavalry wing on their left. Their aim was to occupy

The monument to the Battle of Pinkie, overlooking the battlefield, with Arthur's Seat in the background.

St Michael's Church.

the height on which stood St Michael's Church after which the Scots position could be attacked with artillery from both the fleet and this high point. To Somerset's astonishment the Scots were seen to abandon their defensive position and were crossing the Esk to offer battle on open ground.

The two wings of the Scottish army now suffered from the cavalry on the English left and from the bombardment from the English fleet on the other side. With their wings routed, the Scots centre disintegrated. The Scots lost some 10,000 against not much more than 500 on the English side.

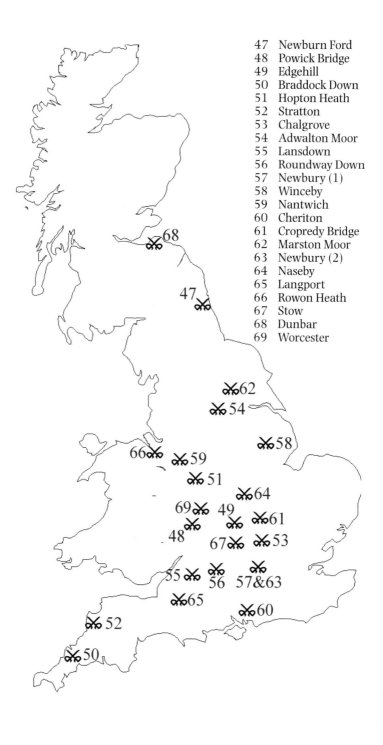

47 Newburn Ford
48 Powick Bridge
49 Edgehill
50 Braddock Down
51 Hopton Heath
52 Stratton
53 Chalgrove
54 Adwalton Moor
55 Lansdown
56 Roundway Down
57 Newbury (1)
58 Winceby
59 Nantwich
60 Cheriton
61 Cropredy Bridge
62 Marston Moor
63 Newbury (2)
64 Naseby
65 Langport
66 Rowon Heath
67 Stow
68 Dunbar
69 Worcester

THE ENGLISH CIVIL WARS

1642-1651

In 1639, Charles I caused dissension in Scotland by trying to impose reform on the Scottish Church. This eventually resulted in a conflict between the Kirk in Scotland and Charles. In 1640, a Scottish army of some 20,000 invaded England and marched on Newcastle. It met and overwhelmed a small English force of 3,500 at Newburn Ford, and then took Newcastle without a shot fired.

Charles was forced to summon a Parliament to raise the funds to buy off the Scots but the irreconcilable differences between Charles and Parliament still remained as to how England should be governed. Ultimately this led to the Civil Wars of 1642–1651. Charles still felt that he had the supreme authority over Parliament and things came to a head when Charles tried and failed in an attempt to arrest certain members of Parliament. He left London for Hull in April 1642 to attempt to gain control of the arms stockpiled there against further threats from the Scots, but was refused entry. Those arms were then sent to London for the use of the Parliamentarian forces and for the rest of the war the Royalists suffered from a dependence on foreign arms.

Charles now formally raised his standard at Nottingham on 22 August, effectively declaring war on Parliament, and then marched to Shrewsbury to connect with his supporters. Parliament had started raising an army in June under the Earl of Essex, who decided to march to Worcester. The first shots of the Civil War were fired at Powick Bridge on 23 September 1642 when a detachment of the Parliamentarians attempted to cut through to Worcester. This was repulsed by Prince Rupert. In the meantime, Charles had started for London, and the Earl of Essex now had to chase hard to catch up. The two armies met at Edgehill where the first real battle took place on 23 October, ending inconclusively.

During 1643, battles were fought at Braddock Down, Hopton Heath, Stratton, Chalgrove, Adwalton Moor, Lansdown, Roundway Down, Newbury and Winceby by various armies of the protagonists throughout the country from Yorkshire to Cornwall with the advantage generally to the Royalists. However, Parliament had by now concluded the Solemn League and Covenant with the Scots,

Execution of Charles I.

who invaded England as their part of the bargain. During 1644, with battles taking place at Nantwich, Cheriton, Cropredy Bridge, Marston Moor and Newbury (again), the results were more even but, ominously for Charles, his defeat at Marston Moor on 2 July 1644 to a huge combined force of English and Scots lost him the north of the country. The Battle of Naseby on 14 June 1645 effectively sealed his fate. A brief flicker of hope for Charles arose with the advent of Montrose, his Lieutenant-General for Scotland, who, within the space of twelve months, defeated all the Scottish armies sent to oppose him, and then threatened to invade England. This, however, came to nought with the defeat of Montrose at Philiphaugh in the Borders. There were further defeats in 1645 for the Royalists at Langport and Rowton Heath and a final defeat at Stow in March 1646. Charles eventually surrendered to the Scots at Newark on 5 May 1646.

Charles escaped to the Isle of Wight in 1647 and entered into an 'Engagement' with the Scots. Broadly, the Scots would change sides in return for a trial period of Presbyterianism in England. But by 1648 Charles was back in the hands of the Parliamentarians, and after a show trial, was executed on 30 January 1649.

The Scots, however, remained true to their agreement, now supporting Charles's son, Prince Charles, and proclaimed him King Charles II. Cromwell marched north to meet this threat and met and defeated the Scots army at Dunbar on 4 September 1650. Cromwell pursued the Scots further into Scotland but was unable to draw them into battle. Eventually, Charles II persuaded his commanders to invade England and make for London. To this end, the Scots marched south as far as Worcester. Here Cromwell caught up with them and the final battle of the Civil Wars was fought on 3 September 1651 with ultimate victory to Cromwell.

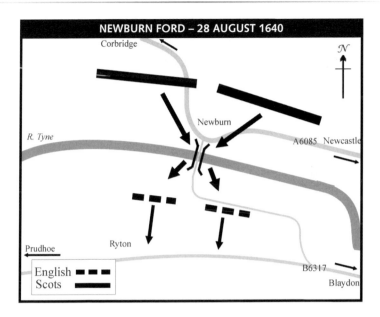

NEWBURN FORD – 28 AUGUST 1640

OS: NZ165651

Newburn is on the A6085 to the east of Newcastle, and the battlefield is immediately to the south of Newburn Bridge which crosses the River Tyne where there was originally a ford, giving the battle its name. Some of the original defensive earthworks can still be seen.

Alexander Leslie, the Earl of Leven, led a Scottish army of some 20,000. He decided to outflank the strong northerly fortifications of Newcastle by crossing the Tyne at Newburn. Lord Conway was the local English leader defending the crossing point but had only 3,500 men at his command. The Scottish cavalry were first to cross the ford and were engaged by the English cavalry. However, although he managed to delay the crossing, Conway faced heavy artillery fire and was heavily outnumbered. He was forced to retreat to the higher ground in the south, leaving the way clear for Leslie to march onto Newcastle, which surrendered without a fight. As a result of this battle King Charles was forced to recall Parliament, which sat throughout the Civil Wars and was known as the Long Parliament. Leslie was later to play an even more important role when he joined his forces with Parliament at Marston Moor.

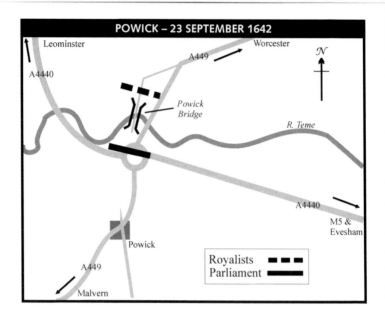

POWICK – 23 SEPTEMBER 1642

OS: SO83X52X

The village of Powick is on the A449 just south of Worcester. The bridge is on the old road and is easy of access. There is good parking at the Mill. Rupert was camped on the north side and, after cutting down the Parliamentarian vanguard, charged across to roll up the remainder.

In September 1642, Worcester had been occupied by Royalist troops, but they were threatened by a large force under the Earl of Essex who was marching from Northampton. Prince Rupert (of the Rhine) decided to evacuate the city and on 19 September led a force of about 1,000 southwards towards Powick Bridge. While he waited there, a Parliamentary force roughly equal to his own attempted to cross the bridge and cut through to Worcester. Rupert waited until their vanguard was across the water and then attacked. The vanguard was overwhelmed and Rupert then charged across the bridge against the remaining forces. They quickly broke and fled. The total time of the skirmish was about fifteen minutes in all and there were few casualties, but the first shots of the Civil War had been fired and the Royalists could claim a notable victory to boost their morale.

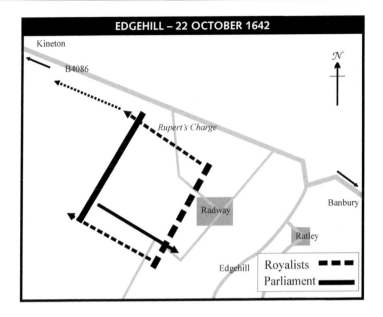

EDGEHILL – 22 OCTOBER 1642

OS: SP354492

The battlefield is almost wholly Ministry of Defence property but a good general view can be obtained from Edgehill itself. Rupert's charge followed what is now the B4086, and there is a monument by the side of this road. There is a battle museum at Farnborough Hall some miles to the south.

Charles I was marching towards London from Worcester and had reached Edgcote by the evening of 22 October when he had news that the Earl of Essex was at Kineton just 11km away. Prince Rupert advised an immediate attack that same day, but Charles decided to site his army in a stronger position and offer battle the next day.

By the early afternoon, the two armies were facing each other, with Essex just south of Kineton and Charles lining the ridge of Edgehill. Neither side appeared willing to commence battle, until a musketeer fired a shot at Charles which fell short. The spot today is known as Bullet Hill. This stirred Charles, who now ordered his forces to descend the hill and line up just north of the village of Radway, with Essex moving forward also.

Two charges by the Royalist cavalry wings demolished their opposing forces, but their impetus carried them off the field of battle. This allowed the Parliamentarian centre and cavalry reserves to regroup and wreak their own damage on the Royalists. Both sides stood off in the evening when the Royalist cavalry returned too

Monument to the battle beside the B4086.

exhausted to take further part. Essex now retreated to Warwick and Charles continued on his way towards Oxford.

Although this first real battle of the Civil War was inconclusive, King Charles could take greater comfort from it than his opponent, the Earl of Essex. Essex's objective had been to interpose himself between the king and London, and this he had signally failed to do. On the other hand Charles now decided to base himself in Oxford, and to that extent he had also failed in his main objective.

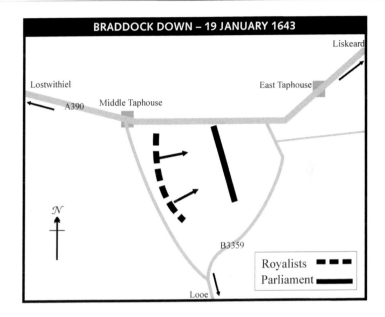

BRADDOCK DOWN – 19 JANUARY 1643

Liskeard

Lostwithiel   East Taphouse

A390   Middle Taphouse

N

B3359

Royalists ▪ ▪ ▪
Parliament ▬▬

Looe

OS: SX177603

The Royalists' line ran south from Middle Taphouse and faced the Parliamentarians lined up to the east. The whole area of the battlefield is now restricted but there is a good view of the battlefield from the minor road leading from the B3359 to the A390. There is a small lay-by for two cars.

Two Parliamentary armies had massed in Devon to attack the Royalists in Cornwall – one under Colonel Ruthin and the other under the Earl of Stamford. Sir Ralph Hopton, in command of the Royalists, decided to face that of Colonel Ruthin before it could meet up with the Earl of Stamford. He marched eastwards and found the Parliamentarians deployed on Braddock Down. The Parliamentarian artillery had not yet reached the main force and Hopton decided to attack immediately. He sent his troops on a charge and the Cornish fighting men swept away the Parliamentarians almost before they could fire a shot in their defence. The leader of the charge was Sir Bevil Grenville, who was to have a monument erected in his memory at Lansdown later in the year. The Parliamentarians retreated in disarray towards Liskeard leaving Cornwall firmly in the hands of the Royalists.

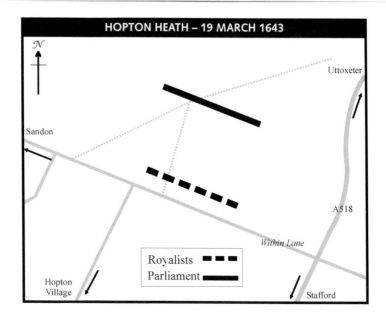

OS: SJ957265

The battlefield is between the A518 and Within Lane just north of the village of Hopton. The Royalists were lined up to the north of the lane facing north-east. Parking is in Hopton at the village hall, with an easy walk along public footpaths right into the heart of the battlefield.

King Charles was concerned about his position in Staffordshire, and accordingly he sent the Earl of Northampton to occupy Stafford and with a force of some 1,200 to stop a Parliamentary advance just north of Stafford at Hopton. The Parliamentarians had been able to choose their position and were on a slight rise in the ground protected by hedges and walls and facing south-west. The Royalists approached late in the afternoon and the battle started with exchanges of artillery fire. Then the Royalists charged, driving back the cavalry of the Parliamentarians but failing to dislodge the infantry. A second charge in the evening routed the Parliamentary cavalry totally, but as darkness fell, both sides withdrew exhausted. During the night the Parliamentarians left the field. The dead numbered about 500, a very high proportion of the numbers taking part.

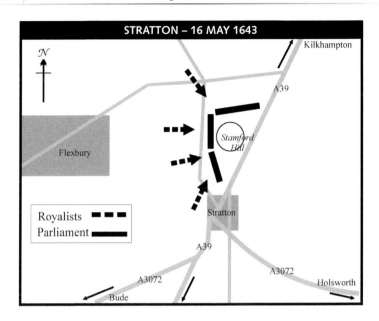

OS: SS227070

Stamford Hill is off the A39 to the north of Stratton. Although they are on private property, access to the earthworks, which formed part of the defence of the Parliamentarians, is allowed by means of a small lay-by and a footpath, which is well signposted. There is a monument at the earthworks.

Sir Ralph Hopton had planned to meet up with Prince Maurice in Somerset, but the Earl of Stamford was determined to foil the plan. He led a force of 5,600 and camped on the steep Stamford Hill just north of Stratton. Hopton's force was only 2,400 with 500 cavalry and he decided to make an attack at dawn by dividing his men into four columns and attacking simultaneously from the north, west and south. The battle raged for several hours inconclusively until James Chudleigh of the Parliamentarians made a counter-charge down the hill in an attempt to smash the Royalists. The Royalist line held, and gradually forced the Parliamentarians back. Now all four columns began to get the upper hand and eventually the four commanders met at the top. When they drove the Parliamentarians off the hill, the Royalist cavalry, until now held in reserve, joined in to seal the victory.

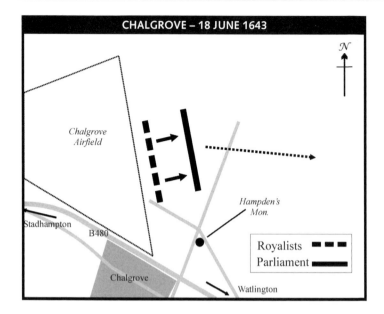

OS: SU645977

The battlefield is just off the B480 outside Chalgrove, and it is possible to walk along public footpaths with views over parts of the battlefield. John Hampden, one of the early important Parliamentarian leaders, was killed at the battle and there is a monument to him.

In the summer of 1643, Charles was based in Oxford with Prince Rupert when news came in that a Parliamentarian pay convoy was expected in the vicinity. Prince Rupert set out to intercept this convoy with a mixed group of cavalry, dragoons and foot soldiers. He was unsuccessful in his search, and eventually decided to retire to Oxford before he was cut off from his base. His pursuers were close behind as he prepared to cross the River Thame at Easington, and he determined to face them at Chalgrove rather than retreat further. The Parliamentarian dragoons were firing at the Royalists from the protection of a hedge and in a moment of quixotic behaviour Rupert spurred his horse to leap the hedge with his own men closely following. After a short, sharp fight the shocked Parliamentarian forces broke and ran.

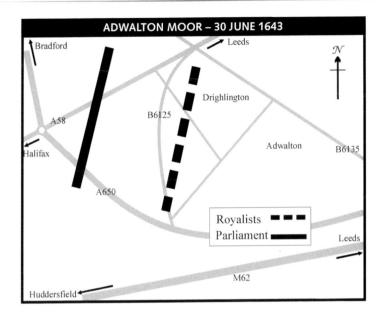

ADWALTON MOOR – 30 JUNE 1643

OS: SE218290

The battlefield is just to the north-east of the A650 with Whitehall Road running right through the middle. The two opposing forces were either side of this road. There is a public right of way running through the heart of the battlefield, crossing from the Royalists to the Parliamentarians.

The Earl of Newcastle was determined to break the power of the Parliamentarians in the north and marched with an army of 10,000 against Bradford. He was met by Fairfax, who decided that as the town could not withstand a siege for long it would be better to give battle. He marched out to Adwalton Moor and built up a strong defensive position on the edge of the moor. The terrain was such that the Royalists were forced to attack at some disadvantage, and initially fortune was with the Parliamentarians. However, the Parliamentarian left then drove forward out of the defences and onto the open moor where the Royalist numerical superiority soon made itself felt and they counter-attacked with pike and cavalry. This was the turning point and the Parliamentarians were overrun. The Royalists now had control of the north, which they were to keep until Marston Moor.

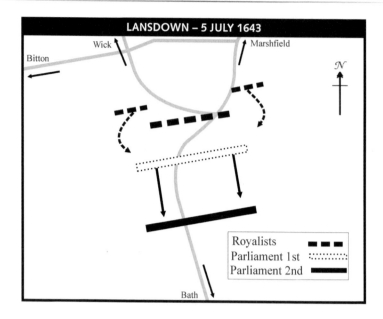

LANSDOWN – 5 JULY 1643

OS: ST723702

Lansdown Hill is about 5km to the north of Bath between the A46 and the A431. The defensive wall that was used by the Parliamentarians as a defence still stands. There is a monument to Sir Bevil Grenville, one of the Royalist leaders killed in the battle, and there are good explanations of the battle.

After the battle at Stratton, Sir Ralph Hopton had effectively gained both Cornwall and Devon for the Royalists and had joined up with Prince Maurice at Chard in Somerset. He now determined to march on Bath with a force of 7,000 and decided to approach the town from the north, where Lansdown Hill was an obvious advantage point. Sir William Waller with a smaller army marched out of Bath and occupied Lansdown Hill before Hopton could get there.

Hopton now had either to retire or to attack this very strong position. He decided on the latter and sent two wings of muskets to attack from the left and the right, with his Cornish Pikes straight up the steep hill in the centre. The cavalry under Prince Maurice also attacked up the centre but slightly to the right where the ground was more open.

The Cornishmen fought their way to the top of the hill which they held despite onslaughts by the Parliamentarians at the severe cost in the death of their leader Sir Bevil Grenville, to whom a monument has been raised where he fell. In the meantime, the left and right

The monument to Sir Bevil Grenville.

wings of muskets gained their objectives, and eventually the ridge was occupied. The Royalist cavalry, starting as 2,000, ended the day as 600 according to Hopton. After a day of bloody fighting, the Royalists had gained the hill, and the Parliamentarians retreated to a stone wall which still exists, but the two sides were too exhausted to continue fighting. During the night the Royalists retreated back to their stronghold in Bath.

The next day, the Royalists suffered two setbacks. In an accident, virtually all their ammunition blew up, and, in the conflagration, Hopton was blinded.

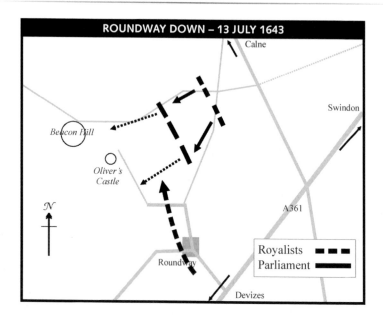

ROUNDWAY DOWN – 13 JULY 1643

OS: SU021655

There is good access to and good parking on Roundway Down at Oliver's Castle, an ancient fortification. Public footpaths cross the site with excellent information on the battle at various points and it is easy walking to see the escarpment and look down upon Bloody Ditch, visualising the carnage.

Following the Battle of Lansdown, Hopton started off to Oxford to join Charles. He arrived at Devizes on 9 July, harried by Waller, who encamped to the north on Roundway Down and laid siege to the town. Having been blinded and wounded at Lansdown, Hopton was confined to bed and was unable to exert the strong leadership that he had shown previously. Since cavalry were useless in a siege, Hopton sent them under Prince Maurice and the Marquis of Hereford to cut their way through, reach Oxford, and ask for help.

This help arrived in the afternoon of 13 July in the shape of 1,800 cavalry under Lord Wilmot. By agreement, Wilmot fired two shots to let Hopton know that he had arrived, but, despite Hopton's strong advice, his brother officers decided not to advance out of the town immediately, and Hopton felt unable to order out his officers while he could not lead them. Thus Wilmot had to face a force nearly twice as large as his own.

Waller, on Roundway Down, lined up his forces to meet this force with his infantry in the centre and two wings of horse. Wilmot, seeing

The escarpment with Bloody Ditch at its foot.

this line-up, decided to ignore the infantry and split his cavalry into two divisions, each attacking a wing of Waller's army. After much charging to and fro, the Royalists gained the upper hand and drove the Parliamentarian cavalry westwards towards a steep escarpment of which neither side was aware. Horses and men tumbled down into what is known as Bloody Ditch. With the sounds of fighting heard in Devizes, Hopton's officers now came round to Hopton's view and marched out of Devizes to join Wilmot. Wilmot, himself, simply circled Waller's dazed infantry, waiting for Hopton, and only when the famous Cornish Pikes appeared did he charge home. The Parliamentarians were completely routed.

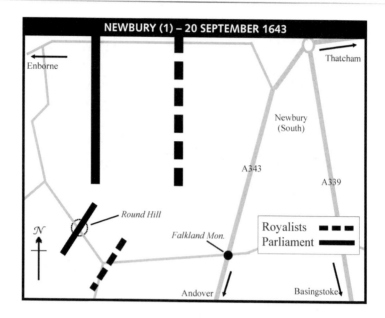

NEWBURY (1) – 20 SEPTEMBER 1643

OS: SU450650

Round Hill, which was the focal point of the battle, is off Cope Hall Lane between the A34 and the A343. There are good footpaths crossing that part of the battlefield, which is still open land. The Falkland Monument on the A343 is right on the line of the Royalists.

The Earl of Essex was striving to reach London from the west and Charles was following in an attempt to intervene. Both were heading for Newbury, and Charles won the race. On 19 September, Charles lined his forces to block the approaches south of the River Kennet and awaited the arrival of the Parliamentarians.

Essex, although realizing that he had lost the race, nevertheless decided to fight it out and sought out a strong defensive position. He managed to occupy Round Hill, which commanded the Royalist position, and for the whole of the next day, battles raged with the main objective of one side or the other winning or holding Round Hill. The Royalists managed to push back the Parliamentarians in the north all the way back to Skinners Green, but were unable to dislodge them from their position on Round Hill.

An artillery duel now developed between the Royalists sited where the Falkland Monument stands and the Parliamentarians on Round Hill, with neither gaining the upper hand. At one stage, Lord

Monument to Lord Falkland and the Royalists who fell in the battle.

Falkland volunteered to try a solitary charge, but was shot down and killed.

Gradually during the day, more and more forces concentrated on both sides at Round Hill, and at the end of the day both sides had suffered substantial losses but neither side could claim absolute victory. During the night, the Royalists fell back to Oxford while Essex was able to achieve his objective and continue on his way to London.

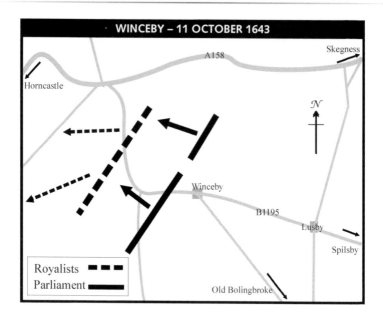

OS: TF314686

The battlefield straddles what is now the B1195 immediately south of the junction with the A158, about 5km east of Horncastle. There is adequate car parking with a public footpath system allowing good views of the battlefield.

Bolingbroke Castle, a Royalist stronghold, was under siege in October, and a Royalist force of cavalry and dragoons was sent out from Lincoln to raise the siege. The Parliamentarians sent out a similar force of cavalry and dragoons to intercept them. They were led by Fairfax with a certain Colonel Oliver Cromwell. The two sides met at Winceby, about three miles north-west of the castle. Cromwell made the initial charge but was wounded and unhorsed in the Royalist counter-charge. Fairfax met this counter-charge with his reserves and made his own charge. In the ensuing muddled fighting, Cromwell was able to find and mount a second horse to rejoin the fray. Within half an hour, the Royalists were put to flight. Many were trapped in Slash Hollow and were killed by the chasing Parliamentarians. Losses on the Parliamentarian side were reportedly light, but with substantial losses suffered by the Royalists.

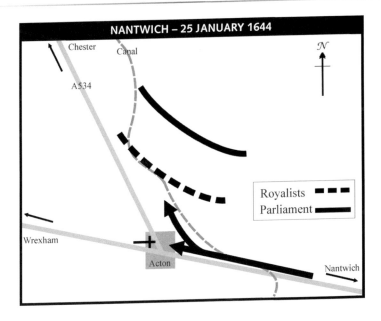

NANTWICH – 25 JANUARY 1644

Chester Canal A534 *N*

Royalists ▬ ▬ ▬
Parliament ▬▬▬

Wrexham

Acton

Nantwich

OS: SJ632531

The battlefield lies in flat open land between the A51 to the north and Acton village, about 1km out of Nantwich. There is a canal, which cuts through the site, but this provides good viewpoints from the crossing bridges. A further excellent viewing point is the tower of Acton Church.

The Parliamentary garrison at Nantwich was being besieged by Lord Byron, when news came in that Sir Thomas Fairfax was marching to its relief with some 5,000 men. Byron decided to withdraw from the siege and meet this threat by marching out to Acton. Fairfax avoided direct fight by by-passing Acton and trying to reach Nantwich from the north and east. Byron wheeled his army so that he could attack the rear and the vanguard at the same time. Fairfax now turned to face Byron and the fighting became ragged and confused. Sheer weight of numbers now began to tell, and Byron was forced back towards Acton and its churchyard. When the Nantwich garrison marched out to join Fairfax and attacked Byron at his rear, the end came after two hours of bloody combat. This defeat led to the end of Charles' hopes of gaining the north-west.

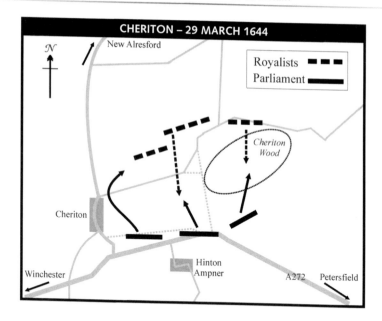

CHERITON – 29 MARCH 1644

OS: SU598293

The battlefield is just to the east of Cheriton and is crossed by paths giving good views. The Royalists faced south with Cheriton Wood to their left and the Parliamentarians were drawn up on the line of Upper Lamborough Lane. Car parking is available in Cheriton.

Sir William Waller had instructions to recapture the West Country and was approaching Winchester from Midhurst. Lord Hopton had gathered new forces and was in Winchester about to try and capture the south-east. As Hopton marched out to Alresford, Waller was encamping at Hinton Ampner about three miles to the south. On 29 March, the two armies met just to the east of Cheriton. Initially the battle favoured the Royalists who managed to eject the Parliamentarians from Cheriton Wood to the Royalists' left and the Parliamentarians' right. At this point it seemed as though the Royalists would win the day, but a reckless charge by one of Hopton's regiment of horse under Sir Henry Bard left him isolated and his regiment completely destroyed. With an original superiority of numbers now accentuated, Waller's forces drove the Royalists from the field forcing Hopton to retreat to Alresford, thus giving up Winchester.

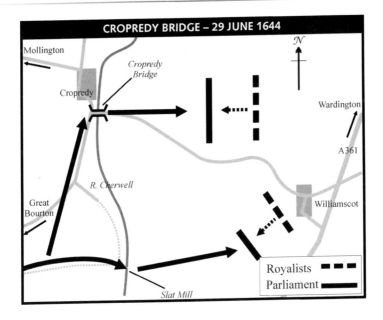

CROPREDY BRIDGE – 29 JUNE 1644

Mollington

Cropredy
Bridge

Cropredy

Wardington

A361

R. Cherwell

Great
Bourton

Williamscot

Slat Mill

Royalists ■ ■ ■
Parliament ■■■■

OS: SP477459

Cropredy Bridge, where Middleton forced his way across, has a plaque recording the battle, and is a good vantage point to visualise the crossing. Slat Mill to the south where Waller attempted a crossing also provides a good vantage point. There are public footpaths crossing the battlefield.

After an abortive attempt to attack Sir William Waller's army at Hanwell, north of Banbury, Charles turned his army north towards Daventry following the east bank of the River Cherwell. Waller matched him by taking the west bank and the two armies marched in parallel in full view of each other.

Charles pushed on towards Hay's Bridge (on the A361) in order to attack a contingent of Parliamentarian cavalry approaching from the north on the west bank of the river. He left a small contingent at the bridge at Cropredy to protect his rear, but his army became so stretched that when he reached Hay's Bridge, his main body was still approaching Wardington under the Earl of Cleveland and the Earl of Northampton, with a further small contingent blocking any pursuit over the bridge at Cropredy.

Waller now saw his own chance to attack and he divided his force. Lieutenant-General John Middleton was to attack the bridge, while he, Waller, would cross an undefended ford at Slat Mill just 1.5km to the south of the village. His force of infantry and cavalry

Above: Cropredy Bridge with the plaque commemorating the battle in the middle of the wall on the right-hand side.

Left: Sir William Waller.

under Middleton soon overcame the Royalists at Cropredy Bridge and crossed the river, advancing towards the Royalist forces spread between Hay's Bridge and Wardington, but he met strong resistance from Cleveland, who forced the Parliamentarians back over Cropredy Bridge.

Waller's own attack against the rear columns of the Royalists under Northampton had faltered, and he was driven back over the ford. Although the Royalists kept up a bombardment against the two defences, no headway could be made, and on the following day Charles marched west towards Evesham.

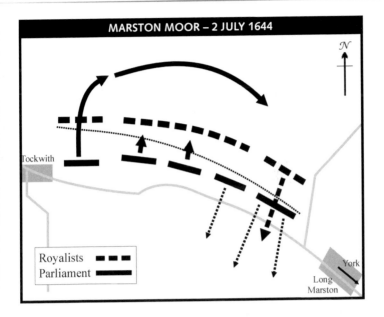

MARSTON MOOR – 2 JULY 1644

Tockwith

Royalists
Parliament

York

Long
Marston

OS: SE491521

The battlefield straddles the road between Tockwith and Long Marston, with the two armies facing each other across the road and stretching almost from one village to the other. There is a monument on the road sited almost in the centre of the battle with good interpretive panels.

In the north, Rupert, with an army of 14,000, had relieved York outmanoeuvring an Allied English Parliamentarian and Scottish force amounting to 27,000. On 2 July he lined up his own army, now increased to 17,000 by the addition of the York garrison under their commander, the Earl of Newcastle, between the villages of Long Marston and Tockwith to face the Allies. Both sides lined up in a traditional format of cavalry wings and central infantry.

By early evening on 2 July, both Rupert and Newcastle decided that nothing more was to happen that day and retired from the field. At that moment the Allies started to advance along their whole front, with Sir Thomas Fairfax leading the charge of the cavalry on the Allied right. Each of the Allied wings met stout resistance and were then pushed back.

On the Royalist left, Lord Goring, with a counter-charge, completely destroyed the Parliamentarian right wing, including the army of Lord Fairfax, leaving Sir Thomas Fairfax stranded and the Scots infantry exposed and surrounded. The Royalist right, after initial

An engraved portrait of Prince Rupert.

An engraved portrait of Oliver Cromwell.

success, were gradually pushed back and then put to flight by the Allied horse under David Leslie, while Cromwell lay wounded. The lines of battle had now slewed round so that the Allied centre, with a numerically superior force, was now facing east and over-lapping the Royalist centre.

At this point in time Sir Thomas Fairfax managed to find his way through the enemy lines to meet up with Cromwell, who had rejoined his dragoons. The two of them now wheeled to their right behind the Royalist infantry and attacked Goring from the rear, relieving the Scots. In the centre, the huge numerical superiority now told against the Royalist infantry who were surrounded and cut to pieces.

Charles had lost the whole of the north of England.

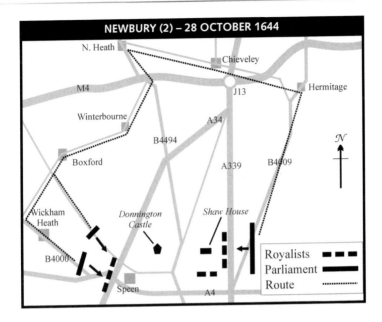

NEWBURY (2) – 28 OCTOBER 1644

Royalists ▪▪▪
Parliament ▪▪▪▪▪
Route ⋯⋯⋯

OS: SU464685
The route taken by the Parliamentarians to attack Speen from the west went via the B4009 to Hermitage then west to Chievely and North Heath, then south-west to Boxford and on to Wickham Heath. Charles's headquarters were at Shaw House, now a school.

In October, Charles was in Newbury with a force of 9,000, having come to the aid of Donnington Castle, while a large Parliamentary army of 19,000 was assembled at Basingstoke. The Parliamentarians decided to strike at Charles immediately and marched to Clay Hill just on the outskirts north-east of Newbury, reaching it in the late afternoon of 26 October. The Royalist forces were based mainly in Speen and Shaw House.

Not liking to attempt an attack against the strong defensive position of the Royalists, the Parliamentarians decided to split their force into two. The Earl of Manchester remained at Clay Hill, while Sir William Waller and Oliver Cromwell went on a long circuitous journey to the west of the town with perhaps two-thirds of the army. Instructions were given that the flanking force was to fire a cannon when they had reached their position. In order to counter this threat, Charles also divided his forces and sent Prince Maurice to occupy Speen.

Although the flanking force was seen by the Royalist garrison at Donnington Castle, no message seems to have been passed to Charles

Donnington Castle.

and by about 3 p.m. on 27 October, the journey was completed and an immediate attack was made on the western defence at Speen.

Two attacks were to have been made simultaneously by Waller and Cromwell, but Cromwell's failed to materialise. Although the Royalists were initially driven out of Speen, a counter-attack drove the Parliamentarians back. The coordinated attack from Clay Hill did not occur until after 4 p.m. by which time it was already dark.

Nightfall soon afterwards brought an end to the fighting with both sides feeling that the day had not gone well, and Charles withdrew to Oxford.

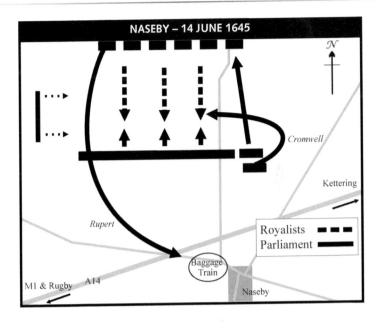

NASEBY – 14 JUNE 1645

Cromwell

Kettering

Rupert

Royalists ■ ■ ■
Parliament ▬▬▬

Baggage Train

M1 & Rugby   A14

Naseby

OS: SP685799

The battlefield is about 1.5km north of Naseby on the Sibbertoft Road. To the left of the road is the Cromwell Monument, right in the middle of the Parliamentarian line. Cromwell's charge, which was so decisive, was on the Parliamentarian right, some 500m to the east of the monument.

The addition of Oliver Cromwell as second in command to Sir Thomas Fairfax meant that the formidable partnership wrought at Marston Moor was now in absolute charge for the first time. Charles was on his way to Market Harborough when Fairfax reached Guilsborough on 13 June. The two armies met just north of the village of Naseby, with the Parliamentarian army nearly twice the size of the Royalists at 14,000 to 7,500.

From the outset, the Royalists made the running and their centre of infantry moved forward to the attack. As soon as the infantry in the centre met, Rupert charged on his right, swept away half of the Parliamentarian right wing and continued on far to the rear of the battle, where his men found the baggage train and wasted no time in engaging with the troops guarding it.

The Royalist centre pushed back the 'New Model Army' almost to the point of flight, until Fairfax brought up his reserves to stop the rot. Half of Cromwell's cavalry on his right now made its own charge, as a mirror image of Rupert's, and drove off the Royalists. The

Monument at the site of the battle.

deciding point came when the remaining Parliamentarian left wing cavalry together with the remainder of Cromwell's right wing turned respectively inwards to surround the Royalist infantry.

The huge numerical superiority now told and by the time that Rupert returned with his cavalry, the battle was over with no hope of recovery.

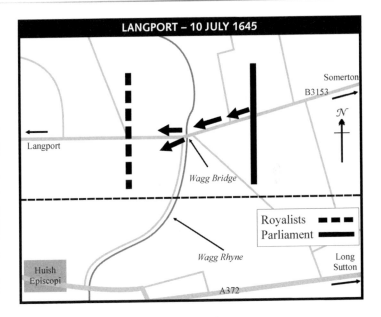

LANGPORT – 10 JULY 1645

Somerton
B3153
N
Langport
Wagg Bridge

Royalists ▬ ▬ ▬
Parliament ▬▬▬

Wagg Rhyne
Long Sutton
Huish Episcopi
A372

OS: ST441275

The charge by the Parliamentarians was along the B3153 Langport-Somerton Road. The original ford is now Wagg Bridge, but better viewpoints can be obtained from the small road which leads from Wagg Bridge to the A372, and from the church tower at Huish Episcopi.

After Naseby, Fairfax's main task was to stop the Royalists in joining up all their scattered forces into one major army that could match the Parliamentarians. In the north, Lord Byron was at Chester while Lord Goring was in the south-west besieging Taunton. Fairfax decided to go after Goring and set off with forced marches towards Taunton. Goring advanced towards Yeovil, but, once again, Fairfax had superiority in numbers and Goring made a decision to withdraw to Bridgewater.

Goring wished to retreat in an orderly manner, but needed time. He therefore decided to send his baggage and artillery first, leaving the remainder of his force and just two of his guns at Langport to cover the retreat. Goring held a very strong defensive position on the Langport side of a stream called the Wagg Rhyne. The only way across was by a ford (now Wagg Bridge) and a narrow road (now the B3153) which could only take four horses abreast.

Fairfax first silenced Goring's artillery then ordered a frontal charge by his cavalry directly across the ford and up the opposite slope. Three

The lane down which Fairfax's cavalry charged to the ford through Wagg Rhyne. The ford has been replaced by Wagg Bridge, the stone parapet of which can be seen in the foreground.

Sir Thomas Fairfax.

troops of horse were detailed as a 'forlorn hope'. Across the ford they charged and up the slope opposite into the middle of Goring's forces. There they were held up and then gradually forced back by sheer weight of numbers towards the river, until reinforcements arrived in the shape of three more troops of horse, this time supported by musketeers. This second charge was more successful and allowed the remainder of the army to cross and eventually put the Royalists to flight.

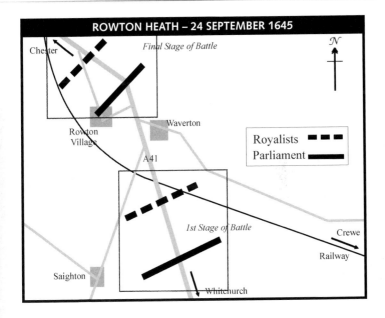

ROWTON HEATH – 24 SEPTEMBER 1645

Chester

Final Stage of Battle

𝒩

Waverton

Rowton
Village

A41

Royalists

Parliament

1st Stage of Battle

Crewe

Railway

Saighton

Whitchurch

OS: SJ454631

The first battle took place across the A41 about 5km south of Chester. The best viewpoint is from the bridge across the railway line just south of the point where it crosses the A41. Charles watched the rout from King Charles Tower on the walls of Chester.

Charles, with his cavalry now under the command of Langdale in the absence of Rupert who had been dismissed, started off to Scotland to join Montrose (see next section) but was persuaded to divert to Chester to relieve the garrison there under siege by the Parliamentarians. Charles had entered Chester, but his army was outside and now itself under attack from a cavalry force of Parliamentarians under Poynitz. The battle that followed lasted all day with initial fortune favouring the Royalists, but later in the day, they were pushed back closer towards Chester. Now the besiegers turned and joined in the battle against Langdale and later on even the garrison of Chester turned out into what was a confusing struggle with no clear lines of demarcation. Finally, the Royalists were defeated, with the king watching from the walls of the city the rout of his beloved cavalry.

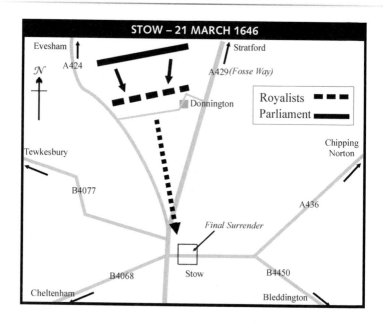

The initial stages of the battle took place at Donnington between the A429 and the A424 about 2km north of Stow. The battle ended in the market square of Stow when Lord Astley, veteran of Newburn (1640), Edgehill (1642) and Naseby (1645), finally surrendered. There is a monument in the square.

By early 1646, Charles' hopes had virtually disappeared with the surrender of Hopton to Fairfax on 12 March and all his standing armies disbanded. His last chance was for foreign troops to come to his rescue, but he needed to hold on to Oxford. Sir Jacob Astley, veteran of Naseby and now in the West Country, was appointed lieutenant-general of all the Royalist forces in the West Country.

Astley was charged with the task of raising an army and fighting his way through to Oxford. If he could do this, Charles calculated that he might be able to hold on until a foreign army came to his aid. Astley, therefore, gathered a motley force of 3,000 and marched east towards Oxford.

Just north of Stow, he met a smaller but more disciplined Parliamentary force under Sir Willian Brereton. Astley occupied the higher ground facing north. The Parliamentarians made the first charge uphill towards the Royalist forces, which first repulsed them and then forced them to retreat in confusion. However, on the right, Sir William Brereton's cavalry made a second and more decisive

A monument to the battle in the market square at Stow.

charge. The Royalists were pushed back and with their cavalry fleeing the field and escaping, the infantry eventually fled all the way into the centre of Stow, where, in the market place, Astley finally surrendered, effectively bringing to a close the first Civil War.

Charles gave himself up to the Scots at Newark on 5 May.

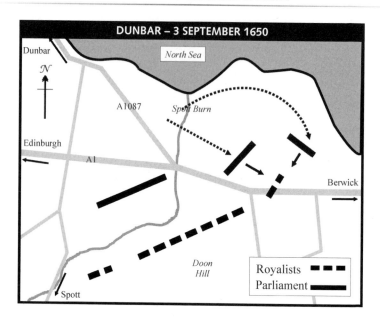

OS: NT697767

Leslie was drawn up on the slopes of Doon Hill stretching for some 2.7km almost to the coast. Cromwell faced him from across the Spott Burn. The attack by Cromwell was on the line of what is now the A1. There is a monument to the battle.

Charles had surrendered in 1646, but had escaped late in 1647. He agreed a deal with the Scots, which brought them back on his side, but by 1649 he had been recaptured and executed. The Scots, however, now recognized his son as Charles II and this prompted an invasion of Scotland by Cromwell in July 1650.

Cromwell's army met a force led by David Leslie near Musselburgh, but found it too strong, and Cromwell retreated to Dunbar. The Scots now advanced to the south of the town and blocked the land route to England. Cromwell, with his smaller force, would either have to fight or escape by sea. On the other hand, Leslie would also need to fight if his opponent were not to slip out of his grasp.

Cromwell, with General John Lambert and General George Monck, studied the Scottish deployment and considered that a concentrated full-scale attack upon the Scottish right would turn the whole army.

In the early hours of 4 September, the English cavalry made a surprise attack on the Scots right. The Scots held firm until Cromwell in a flanking movement attacked them from the side and rolled them up. Leslie's army now disintegrated and fled the field. Victory for Cromwell was complete.

Monument to the battle close to the A1.

The Seal of Charles II.

A footnote: General Monck (later Duke of Albemarle) fought for Charles I then served the Parliamentarians until 1660, and in that year helped in the restoration of Charles II to the throne.

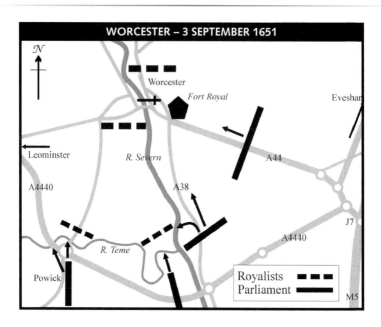

WORCESTER – 3 SEPTEMBER 1651

OS: SO858453

There are three major viewpoints of the battle. The Cathedral Tower (for a long-distance general view south), the junction of the River Severn and the River Teme, where the pontoon bridges were built, and just off the A4440, where it crosses the Severn. At this latter point there is an interpretive panel.

After Dunbar, Cromwell pursued the Scots further into Scotland but was unable to bring them to battle. David Leslie gradually increased his numbers, and eventually Charles II decided to make for London. He decided to go by the west route to try and pick up supporters from Wales and the West Country, and he reached Worcester on 22 August.

Cromwell made a series of forced marches to cut him off from London, and now approached Worcester from the east and the south with an army of 28,000 against Charles's 16,000. General John Lambert was despatched to gain the bridge at Upton, thus allowing the Parliamentarians to approach Worcester from the south on both banks of the River Severn. The Royalists pulled back into Worcester and also manned the north bank of the River Teme.

The Royalist position was strong and now defended by two rivers, the Severn and the Teme. Cromwell solved the problem of the rivers by constructing two pontoon bridges, which would allow him to advance to the city both by the east and west bank of the Severn. These were made at Upton and dragged upstream under the command of General Charles Fleetwood to be placed one over the Severn and other across the Teme. Fleetwood attacked across the Teme to clear the ground immediately opposite the sites for the bridges. Cromwell now poured his troops into the eastern meadows to join Fleetwood.

Seeing this, Charles seized the opportunity to counter-attack the Parliamentarians besieging Fort Royal. Cromwell was forced to withdraw a substantial number of his troops from the east side of the river in order to push back the Royalists. Unfortunately for Charles, David Leslie did not budge from his position to the north of Worcester, whether by design or accident, and Charles did not have sufficient numbers to keep up the attack once Cromwell reappeared.

As darkness fell, the Scottish cavalry fled the city, leaving the infantry to their fate. The Royalists were utterly defeated and Charles had to flee the country.

Plaque at the centre of Worcester commemorating the escape of Charles II after the battle.

70 Aberdeen
71 Inverlochy
72 Auldearn
73 Alford
74 Kilsyth

THE CIVIL WAR IN SCOTLAND

1644-1645

When Civil War broke out in England, both the English Parliament and the king sought the aid of the General Assembly in Scotland, still as yet a separate country but sharing the same sovereign with England. Because of the religious differences then hardening, it gradually became clear that the king could expect no assistance from this quarter, and eventually, in 1643, the Solemn League and Covenant was entered into by the General Assembly and Estates in Scotland and Parliament in England. The Kirk and nobility of Scotland had at this moment in time sealed their hypocrisy. Within this Solemn League and Covenant they vowed to 'preserve and defend the king's majesty's person and authority'. Nothing could have been further from the truth. This was the moment at which Scotland finally declared open rebellion against its king. This Covenant ensured that the ruling bodies in Scotland would henceforth support Parliament against their king.

Not all in Scotland agreed with this action, however, and the king still had hopes of raising an army there to come to his aid in the south.

The stage was set for the entry into military history of James Graham, the Marquis of Montrose, and newly appointed lieutenant-general of the king, who was to mould the disparity of the Highland and Irish clans into an experienced fighting machine and defeat all the armies sent against him by the Estates in six major battles

An engraved portrait of James Graham, Marquis of Montrose.

all fought within a space of twelve months. He joined Alasdair MacDonald with his 1,600 Irish and Highlanders at Blair, and with this small band set out to conquer Scotland for his king. At Tippermuir (1 September 1644) he and his forces heard for the first time that dreadful battle cry of the Covenanters, 'Jesus and no quarter!' At Aberdeen (13 September 1644), Montrose was so incensed by the wanton shooting in the back of a small drummer-boy, who was only accompanying an envoy under a flag of truce, that he promised his men the sack of Aberdeen after they had won.

From Aberdeen, Montrose went by devious routes to Inverary, which he sacked in December. Leaving Inverary in mid-January, he marched north to meet Seaforth at Inverness, but when he reached Kilcummin on 29 January, he received news that Argyll with his army of some 3,000 Campbells was just thirty miles to his rear. Montrose decided to turn round and meet this threat first. He met and defeated the Campbells at Inverlochy (2 February 1645). His victory at Auldearn (9 May 1645) has graced books on military strategy ever since. His main idea was to accept immense pressure on his right wing, and hit his opponents sideways on by a hinging movement with his left. This was followed by Alford (2 July 1645) where Montrose defeated Baillie. Montrose then spent the next three months recruiting and preparing to march south at last to the assistance of King Charles. By mid-August he had mustered 4,400 infantry and 500 cavalry – by far the largest force he had commanded. Baillie, back in favour again after Alford, had about 6,000 foot and 600 horse. They met again at Kilsyth (15 August). In the ensuing battle, Baillie's forces were routed and slaughtered unmercifully.

Montrose was now master of Scotland, but his aim to bring a Scottish army to the aid of his king was never to be fulfilled. As soon as he marched south of the Highlands, he found that the clans were as fickle as ever, and they deserted him in droves to return to their valleys and mountains. On 13 September at Philiphaugh, with only 500 of his loyal Irish and 100 troopers with him facing 6,000, Montrose was ambushed and utterly beaten. He was persuaded against his will that the cause was greater than the individual and he fled to France.

True to their dreadful battle cry, the Covenant leaders, having given guarantees of quarter to the defeated army, simply murdered them as soon as they surrendered.

Montrose returned in 1650 and landed in the north of Scotland, but without his Irish and Highland clans he was unable to repeat his magic and was finally defeated at Carbisdale.

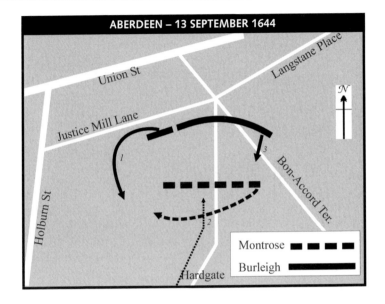

ABERDEEN – 13 SEPTEMBER 1644

Union St

Langstane Place

Justice Mill Lane

Holburn St

Bon-Accord Ter.

Montrose ■ ■ ■ ■
Burleigh ▬▬▬▬

Hardgate

OS: NJ935058

The battlefield stretched across what is now Hardgate. This lane continuing via Langstane Place was the main road to old Aberdeen. The attempted flanking movement by the Covenanters was west along Justice Mill Lane and then south towards the rear of Montrose's left wing.

Montrose had marched by various ways from Perth to Dundee and then to the hills of Angus, where he heard of the presence of Lord Burleigh with an army in Aberdeen. He reached the Dee Valley and peacefully occupied Crathes Castle on 11 September. Next day he marched to Aberdeen by the north bank of the Dee, coming up against Burleigh just 3km from Aberdeen.

On the morning of 13 September, Montrose sent an envoy accompanied by a drummer-boy to the magistrates of the city asking them to surrender, or send away the women and children. The magistrates received the envoy courteously but declined the offer. As the two were returning, the little boy was shot in the back by one of Burleigh's soldiers. In anger, Montrose promised Alasdair MacDonald the sack of the city, and prepared for battle.

The two sides straddled a lane on a line of the present Hardgate, which led from the city to the River Dee. Montrose's force consisted of about 1,500 Irish infantry, now adequately armed, and some seventy horse. The Covenanters had about 2,000 infantry and 500 horse.

Bon Accord Crescent Gardens between Hardgate and Bon Accord Terrace, site of the Battle of Aberdeen.

A plaque in Aberdeen recalling the battle of 1644.

An initial manoeuvre by the Covenant to outflank Montrose's left (1 on the map) was repulsed by a rapid switch of all Montrose's cavalry to his left wing (2). Although this realignment enabled him to counter the danger, it weakened his right and allowed his opponents on that wing to make their charge (3). The Irish infantry withstood the onslaught until Montrose's victorious cavalry returned from his left. This was the deciding point of the battle. A general advance and charge by the Irish broke the Covenanters and the battle was won.

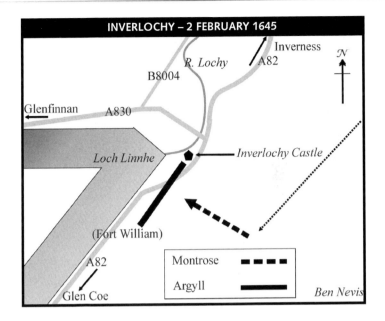

INVERLOCHY – 2 FEBRUARY 1645

Inverness
R. Lochy
A82
B8004
N

Glenfinnan   A830

Loch Linnhe   Inverlochy Castle

(Fort William)

A82   Montrose ■ ■ ■ ■

Argyll ▬▬▬

Glen Coe   Ben Nevis

OS: NN104734

The battle took place initially where Argyll's forces were camped in the immediate vicinity of the old castle. It then spread to the bank of the river and then to the loch and for a few miles downstream.

In the months September to November, Montrose marched up and down the Highlands, always seeking more support, but none came. Worse, Alasdair MacDonald now took with him his Highlanders to the west, ostensibly in search of recruits, but probably to carry booty home and to see to the security of his own stronghold, leaving Montrose with little more than 800 infantry. But in November, Alasdair returned with levies from all the Highland clans, giving Montrose an army of some 3,000. The clans were looking for a fight – not with the Covenant, but with the Campbells, the ancient enemy.

Montrose led his force from Blair to Inveraray, and sacked the Campbell capital, plundering it for a few weeks before retreating north. At Kilcummin (Fort Augustus) on Loch Ness he learned that Argyll was now chasing him with an army of 3,000 while ahead was Lord Seaforth in Inverness with some 5,000. His own army was now reduced to 1,500, with the customary desertions of Highlanders to their homes. Montrose decided to return to meet Argyll.

Ruins of the old Inverlochy Castle round which the battle took place.

Early on the morning of 31 January 1645 Montrose took his little army into the hills in order not to allow Argyll's scouts to learn of his whereabouts, and in the depths of winter marched them through the snow and over trackless moors from Kilcummin to reach the outskirts of Inverlochy by the evening of 1 February, to be ready for battle on the next morning. The surprise was complete. There were no tactics. Montrose ordered a charge almost at once. The Lowlanders in the Campbell army gave way very quickly, and although Clan Campbell stood fast and fought fiercely, the MacDonalds and Camerons, inveterate foes of the hated Campbells, were not to be denied. While Lowlanders who were caught were given quarter, none was given to the Campbells. Some 1,500 of them were slaughtered during the rout and the military power of Clan Campbell was gone forever.

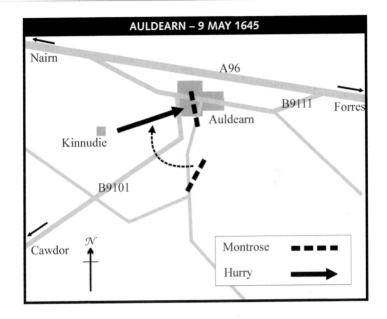

AULDEARN – 9 MAY 1645

Nairn

A96

B9111   Forres

Auldearn

Kinnudie

B9101

Cawdor   *N*

Montrose ▪ ▪ ▪ ▪

Hurry ➤

OS: NH917550

Hurry approached from Kinnudie and MacDonald's defensive line stretched south from Castle Hill (now the Dovecot). Montrose kept all his horse and the rest of his infantry hidden behind a ridge running north-east/south-west. At the right moment they charged on the unsuspecting right of Hurry.

Three months after the Battle of Inverlochy, in the evening of 8 May, Montrose was at Auldearn on the trail of Sir John Hurry. For all that time he had been criss-crossing the Highlands, sometimes the hunter, sometimes the quarry, and now Hurry was withdrawing to Inverness, and Montrose meant to catch him there. Hurry, however, had been laying a trap for Montrose, intending to draw him out of his beloved hills.

During the night of 8/9 May, Hurry turned unexpectedly. Montrose's scouts gave warning, and Montrose immediately knew what was happening. At dawn, he drew up his defences.

He placed 400 Irish and Highland foot under Alasdair MacDonald as a weak right wing in a very strong defensive position, gave them his royal standard, and put a few muskets in the village gardens as a false centre with orders to keep up continuous firing. All his horse and the rest of his infantry he kept hidden behind a ridge to the south.

His tactics all depended on his right being able to hold off odds of about six-to-one for sufficient time to allow Sir John Hurry to devote

View looking south over the battlefield from the Dovecote on Castle Hill.

all his forces in attacking MacDonald in the belief that Montrose was there in person. The idea was for his cavalry to sweep round the hill and crash unexpectedly into the right wing of his opponents. The plan very nearly failed because of an impetuous charge by MacDonald, but a well-disciplined retreat to their defences enabled the Irish and Highlanders to hold off their opponents.

Montrose could see that MacDonald's situation was deteriorating all the time and gave the word for his Gordon cavalry to make their charge. The shock of this sent Hurry's troops reeling and at the same time, Major Drummond, commanding Hurry's right wing of cavalry, gave the wrong order to his men to wheel to the left instead of the right. Montrose then sent in his reserves, and MacDonald called on his men to make one more charge; Hurry's army collapsed. The northern levies fled, leaving the brunt of the attack to the regular regiments. The final pursuit lasted for 20km.

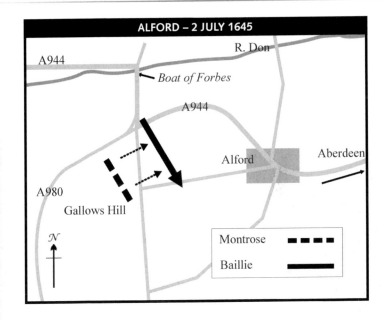

ALFORD – 2 JULY 1645

R. Don

A944

Boat of Forbes

A944

Alford

Aberdeen

A980

Gallows Hill

𝒩

| Montrose | ■ ■ ■ ■ |
| Baillie | ▬▬▬ |

OS: NJ565165

Montrose occupied Gallows Hill just to the south of the ford known as Boat of Forbes (now Bridge of Alford). Baillie crossed the river to reach Woodend, where the A944 meets the A980, before he realised the strength of Montrose's army. Baillie was caught with marshes between his army and the river.

Just east of the Muir of Alford, Montrose placed his army facing north-east on the upper slopes of Gallows Hill while Baillie was still marching south towards the River Don. To approach Montrose's position, Baillie had to cross the Don by the ford at Boat of Forbes, and then cross marshy fields. He could only see part of Montrose's force and thought that he was only attacking the rearguard of a much larger force. Instead of a frontal attack, he decided to outflank his opponent by marching to the east of Gallows Hill. It was only when he had forded the river and had started his outflanking movement that he realised his mistake. Before he had a chance to change his mind, the Royalist cavalry swept down the hill, and battle was joined. Baillie was caught with his back to the marshes, had nowhere to retreat, and was utterly crushed.

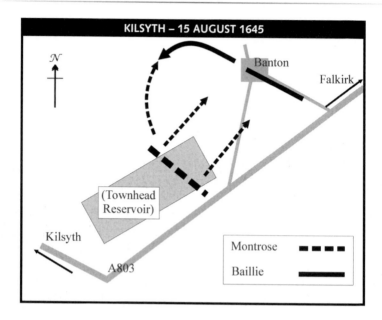

KILSYTH – 15 AUGUST 1645

N

Banton

Falkirk

(Townhead Reservoir)

Kilsyth

A803

| Montrose | ▬ ▬ ▬ ▬ |
| Baillie | ▬▬▬▬▬ |

OS: NS741787

Montrose was camped in a meadow (now the Townhead Reservoir). Baillie tried to outflank Montrose by marching along the rim towards the homestead of Auchinvalley. Montrose counter-attacked first against the column's head and then against the centre, cutting Baillie's forces in two.

Montrose was still determined to take an army south to the aid of his king, but time after time, his Highlanders and cavalry deserted him, returning to their homes. They had no desire to cross the 'border' into the Lowlands, let alone the border into England. But now, in August, Montrose had some 4,400 foot and over 400 cavalry joining his banner, and he felt at last that the time was right for a venture south. Then he learned that not only was Baillie at Perth with 6,000 men but there was a further Covenanting army in the west under Lanark marching to join up with Baillie. On 10 August, Montrose resolved to interpose himself between the two armies and marched west to Stirling. By the evening of 14 August he was camped in a hollow in a meadow just north-east of Kilsyth. That same evening, Baillie was camped just 5km away from Montrose.

On the morning of 15 August, Baillie marched out to meet Montrose and found himself on a ridge (where the modern township of Banton is situated) looking down upon

Townhead Reservoir from Auchinvalley.

Montrose's camp. In order to attempt an encirclement of Montrose, Baillie now set out to march along the rim across Montrose's front in a north-westerly direction. While he was engaged in this manoeuvre, Montrose sent a party to secure his left at Auchinvalley.

This outpost was attacked by the vanguard of Baillie, and this in turn provoked a counter-attack by Alasdair MacDonald and his Irish and Highlanders. These now charged uphill and cut the Covenant force in two. While Macdonald destroyed the centre, Montrose's cavalry routed the van. It was now that Montrose ordered a general advance up the hill. The fighting lasted several hours, but as soon as it was clear to Baillie that the day was lost, he made his escape, leaving his men to the fury of the Irish and Highlanders. Only two weeks before the battle, a company of Covenanters had come across some of the womenfolk of the Irish at Methven Wood and had butchered them out of hand. The memory of this was still fresh, and no quarter was given to Baillie's men. Of the 6,000 Covenanters who started the day only a few hundred survived. The leaders of the Covenanting army all escaped, as was the custom, because they had the better horses, and did not scruple to desert the simple men who trusted them. The western army under Lanark never reached the battlefield and escaped the slaughter.

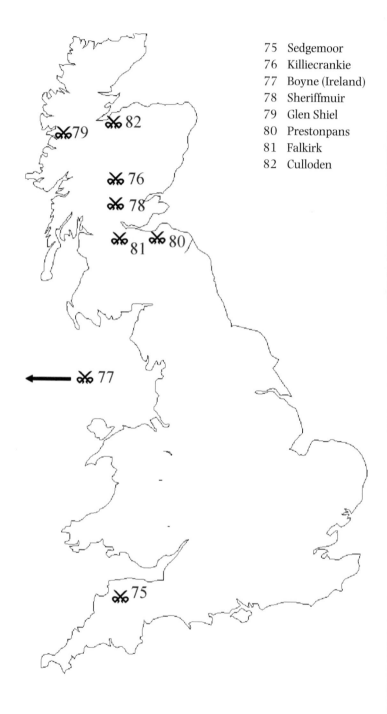

75 Sedgemoor
76 Killiecrankie
77 Boyne (Ireland)
78 Sheriffmuir
79 Glen Shiel
80 Prestonpans
81 Falkirk
82 Culloden

REBELLIONS

Charles II was restored to the throne of England in 1660, and the country was relatively peaceful until he died in 1685, apart from skirmishing in Scotland between non-conformists and the Government. On Charles's death, James, Duke of Monmouth, the illegitimate son of Charles II, took up arms against Charles' brother James, who had been proclaimed King James II. Monmouth landed at Lyme Regis on 11 June and called to his banner typical West Country nonconformists who rebelled against the Papist ways of the king. The army of James II and Monmouth met at Sedgemoor with a crushing defeat for the rebels and a witch hunt afterwards. Monmouth was executed on 15 July 1685.

By 1688, Parliament had had enough of James's Catholicism, and had invited William of Orange (William III), nephew of James II, to reign jointly with his wife Mary (Mary II), daughter of James II. James by this time had fled the country, thus allowing Parliament to declare that he had abdicated, but he still had his followers in Scotland.

In April 1689, the first 'Jacobite Rebellion' in support of James II was initiated by John Graham of Claverhouse, Viscount Dundee, who led his forces to victory over the Scottish Government forces in July 1689, at Killiecrankie. However, that rebellion was short-lived and was over by the next year. In 1690, James II returned to Ireland for support. William decided to meet this challenge himself and the two sides met at the River Boyne on 1 July 1690. William, at the head of his army, defeated James II, giving rise to the annual celebrations of the protestant 'Orange Order' in Ulster.

Following the deaths of William and Mary without an heir, the crown passed to Mary's sister, Anne, but in 1714 she also died childless. With the Act of Union passed in 1707, Parliament now had a serious problem of succession. James II had died in 1701, leaving a son, also called James Stuart, by his second wife, but Parliament determined not to have the Stuarts back at any cost. They therefore invited George, Elector of Hanover, great-grandson of James VI and I, and, most importantly, a Protestant, to become a constitutional

Statue of Bonnie Prince
Charlie in Derby.

king with no powers of rule. This led to the second Jacobite Rebellion
in support of James Stuart (the 'Old Pretender') as 'James III', with
battles at Sheriffmuir and Glen Shiel, but in both cases the Jacobites
had the worst of the fighting.

There was a third and final Jacobite Rebellion in 1745, when the
son of James Stuart, the 'Old Pretender', now claimed the throne.
This was the romantic figure of Charles Edward Stuart, the 'Young
Pretender', styled 'Charles III', and known to history as 'Bonnie
Prince Charlie'. Charles raised his standard at Glenfinnan on 19
August, and, gathering support as he went, marched on and occupied
Edinburgh. The army of the Government (the Hanoverians) had
mistaken his intentions and were left stranded in the Highlands.
They sailed from Aberdeen to Dunbar and marched towards
Edinburgh to meet the rebels. The armies met at Prestonpans with
a resounding victory for the Jacobites. Charles now determined to
march on London, but, through lack of English support, had to halt
his advance at Derby and return to Scotland. He met and defeated
another Government army in January 1746 at Falkirk, but then the
Hanoverians were strengthened with a new leader, William, Duke of
Cumberland. Charles retreated into the Highlands and the two armies
met at Culloden on 16 April 1746. This, the last battle to be fought in
Britain, saw with utter finality the Jacobite dream shattered.

In honour of his victory, Cumberland had a composition written
for him by Handel, *See the conquering hero comes*, and had a flower
named after him: 'Sweet William'. By the clansmen he was viewed
somewhat differently and was called after a particularly obnoxious
weed: 'Stinking Willie'!

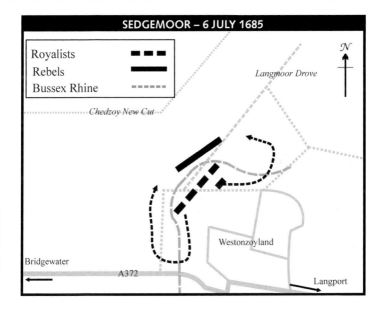

SEDGEMOOR – 6 JULY 1685

Royalists
Rebels
Bussex Rhine

Langmoor Drove

Chedzoy New Cut

Westonzoyland

Bridgewater

A372

Langport

OS: ST352357

The battlefield is on the northern outskirts of Westonzoyland. The Royalists camped south of the Bussex Rhine (now filled in) and the rebels approached from the north. A monument is situated in the centre of the battle and is in easy walking from Bussex Farm where there is car parking.

James, Duke of Monmouth, landed at Lyme Regis on 11 June 1685, and, collecting an army from scratch, marched first to Bristol and then to Bath, eventually retreating to Bridgewater which he entered on 3 July. His morale was low because he had not been given the support he assumed was his, and a rising in Scotland had failed. The Royalists, following him in a relaxed manner, eventually reached Westonzoyland on 5 July, where they camped to the south-east of the Bussex Rhine.

The Earl of Feversham, the Royalist commander, placed 150 troops in Chedzoy as an outpost against a night attack, and a patrol under Colonel Oglethorpe to Bawdrip. Monmouth learned of all this as he was about to set off for Bristol again, but now changed his mind and determined on a night attack against the Royalist forces near Westonzoyland. He had superiority in numbers but his army was ill-trained and poorly armed, as against what was probably the best small army in the country.

View over Sedgemoor, with the 'Stone of Memory' on the right.

He marched from Chedzoy on a roundabout route to avoid the Royalist outposts, with the most stringent orders about absolute silence. One of the orders was that anyone making a noise was to be stabbed by his neighbour! Monmouth reached the Royalist camp in the early hours of 6 July, but the element of surprise had been lost. A scout had heard them as they passed Chedzoy, and had roused the garrison there.

A solitary trooper was sent post haste to the camp at Bussex Rhine to warn them and then return to Chedzoy. The garrison at Chedzoy now galloped at speed to cut off the rebels. There was a confused meeting outside the camp which by now was fully roused. Some of Monmouth's cavalry turned to the right across the face of the defences and some turned left and met the Chedzoy troops now standing guard.

When James eventually reached the camp he decided on a night fire-fight at a distance, eventually running out of ammunition.

At dawn the Royalists first advanced on both flanks and then in the centre, rolling up the rebels and forcing Monmouth to flee the battlefield. There is a monument in the battlefield, next to Langmoor Drove, called the 'Stone of Memory'.

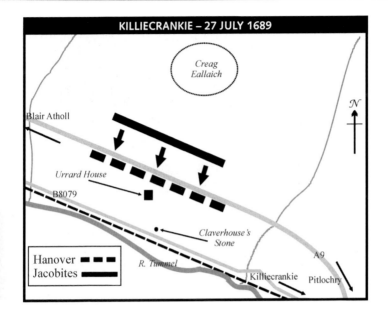

KILLIECRANKIE – 27 JULY 1689

Creag Eallaich

N

Blair Atholl

Urrard House

B8079

Claverhouse's Stone

Hanover ■ ■ ■
Jacobites ■■■■

R. Tummel

A9

Killiecrankie   Pitlochry

OS: NN902636

The A9 drives right through the middle of the battlefield about 2km north of Killiecrankie near the township of Aldclune. There is a memorial stone (Claverhouse's Stone) on the site and a Scottish National Trust Visitor Centre in Killiecrankie giving excellent information on the battle.

John Graham of Claverhouse, Viscount Dundee and commander of James II's forces in Scotland, had been declared a rebel by the Scottish Parliament in 1689 when they offered the throne of Scotland to William and Mary in place of James II. In response, Dundee raised the standard of King James and thus inaugurated the first Jacobite Rebellion. The Scottish Parliament appointed General Hugh Mackay commander-in-chief of the Government forces.

Dundee deemed it vital to his interests that Blair Atholl be held for the Jacobites, and, late at night on 26 July, entered Blair Castle. He held an immediate council of war at which it was decided to attack Mackay the next day, even though Mackay's force was nearly twice as large. In the meantime Mackay also set out for Blair and reached Dunkeld by 26 July. At dawn he marched out of Dunkeld, reached Pitlochry by 10 a.m. and had cleared the pass of Killiecrankie by 3 p.m. Mackay chose to use Urrard House as his headquarters and waited for his army to close up.

Claverhouse's Stone on the site of the Battle of Killiecrankie.

Dundee was seen to be marching down the valley of the Clune towards Aldclune but then he swung to the left to face Mackay's forces, which by now had advanced to the north of Urrard House, but still had the lower ground and the River Garry at their backs. Mackay later wrote in his memoirs that the initiative was with Dundee, for he, Mackay, could receive the enemy, but not attack them.

Dundee waited until evening to lessen the glare of the sun in his men's faces, and at 8 p.m., with the sun now setting behind Beinn Dearghe, sent his Highlanders on a charge down from their advantageous high ground to scatter the Government forces. During the fighting Dundee was killed. Of the 4,300 combatants, 1,900 were killed, over one third.

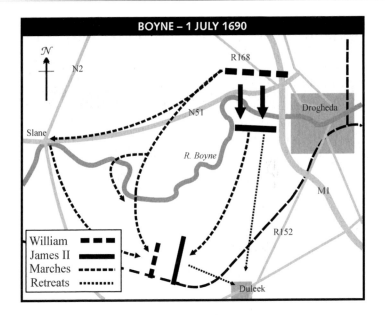

BOYNE – 1 JULY 1690

OS: O0475 (IRELAND)

The battlefield is off the N51 just to the west of the M1 (Ireland) at J10, about 2.5km from Drogheda. There is an excellent visitor's centre at the battlefield with good parking. William's forces were on the north bank and James's on the south. A bridge now exists where originally there was a ford at Oldbridge.

Having fled from England, James II set about raising an army to recover his kingdom. He sailed from France for Kinsale, Ireland, in 1689, and within two weeks was in Dublin. On 14 June 1690, the new king, William III, landed at Carrickfergus in Ulster and immediately set out for Dublin. By 30 June at the River Boyne, he met the forces of James II. James had left some 1,300 troops in Drogheda, and now had 23,000 facing William's 36,000.

At dawn on 2 July, William sent 10,000 men under Count Meinhard Schomberg and General James Douglas a few miles upstream towards Slane with the intention of crossing the river both at Slane and Rosnaree and attacking James's left wing from the side. James tried to defend his position by sending a substantial force to meet this threat, but the result was that he denuded his centre, giving William a huge numerical superiority at the Oldbridge ford. The two battles were now fought out at Roughgrange, just south of Rosnaree, and between Oldbridge and Drybridge. William himself crossed at Drybridge.

Cannons at the site of the Battle of the Boyne.

Eventually William's forces prevailed and the Jacobites were forced to retreat to Duleek. James, fleeing the field, was first to arrive back in Dublin with the news.

The battle was significant and with peculiar features. It was fought out between two crowned kings of England – but in a foreign field. William, as a staunch Protestant, was seen to be fighting against the return of Catholicism in England, but was supported by the Pope as part of the Grand Alliance against Louis XIV of France. William, normally a reserved man, showed great valour, while James, with a soldier's reputation, remained outside the battle and was first off the field. The result fixed William firmly on the throne of England as a constitutional monarch.

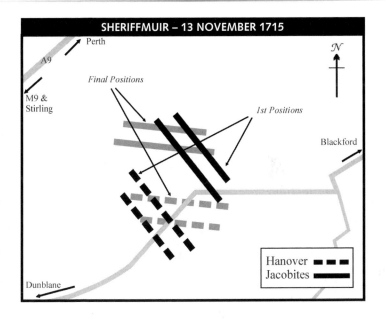

SHERIFFMUIR – 13 NOVEMBER 1715

OS: NN829028

The battlefield is about 10km north of Stirling and 3km out of Dunblane on a minor road to Blackford. There is a memorial cairn to the Clan Macrae at the site. The knowledge of the Earl of Mar's political changes of heart gave rise to his nickname 'Bobbing John'.

The Jacobite standard had been raised for a second time by John Erskine, Earl of Mar, at Braemar on 6 September 1715, and he quickly raised an army to support his cause. He sent a detachment to the north of England to gather support there and then waited in Perth for developments.

By 10 November, he decided that he needed to march south and set off for Dunblane. His antagonist, the Duke of Argyll, reacted quickly and marched north to occupy Dunblane before Mar. This he did and then marched north to meet the rebels on Sheriffmuir although outnumbered by three to one.

Each army's right wing found itself overlapping the other so that when Mar's right wing suddenly charged, their left wing was stranded. Then when Mar's left wing itself made an undisciplined charge, they were halted and then thrown back by Argyll's right wing which was able to attack them from the side.

As Mar's right wing started to gain the upper hand, so did that of Argyll. Gradually the whole army of each slewed round so that while Argyll was now well north of his original position, Mar was moving

Memorial cairn to the Clan Macrae beside the road at Sheriffmuir.

south towards Stirling, and the original battlefield was almost deserted. Both leaders drew back to the battlefield, but both lines held off until dark, even though Mar still hugely outnumbered Argyll.

With no conclusive outcome Argyll had accomplished his task. Mar did not occupy Dunblane. His lack of leadership and indecision had failed his side.

One Highlander exclaimed in frustration: 'Oh, for an hour of Dundee.'

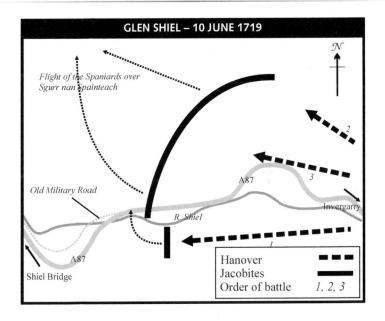

GLEN SHIEL – 10 JUNE 1719

Flight of the Spaniards over Sgurr nan Spainteach

N

Old Military Road

A87

R. Shiel

Invergarry

Shiel Bridge

A87

Hanover	- - -
Jacobites	▬▬▬
Order of battle	*1, 2, 3*

OS: NG991134
The battlefield is on the A87 Invergarry to Kyle of Lochalsh road about 11km south of Shiel Bridge at the head of Loch Duich. The Jacobites had the river on their right and a ravine on their left, and had thrown up entrenchments and barriers across the road.

A third Jacobite uprising started in 1718, with the support of Spain. An agreement was reached whereby a small Spanish force of 300 would land on the west coast of Scotland and would meet up with rebel Highlanders. While this force led by George Keith, Earl Marischal, and the Marquess of Tullibardine acted as a diversion, the main Spanish army would invade southern England with some 5,000 well-armed troops under the command of James Butler, Duke of Ormonde, supported by twenty-nine ships.

The two forces set sail but the larger fleet was destroyed by a storm and never reached its destination, leaving the smaller force to continue unaware of the disaster. They landed at the head of Loch Alsh in April and soon found their position desperate. Little or no help had been forthcoming from the clans, and the Royal Navy began to attack their base in Eilean Dolan Castle. Added to these problems, General Wightman with a strong Government force was marching from Inverness. In order to avoid being trapped, the rebels were forced to march up Glen Shiel before they were ready and set up a blockade about 11km south of Shiel Bridge. The Spaniards formed the rebels'

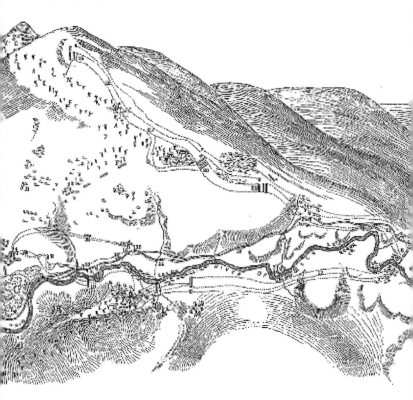

A plan of the field of the battle drawn on the spot by Lieutenant John Bastide, an officer in General Wightman's army. The authors are grateful to the Society of Antiquaries of Scotland for permission to reproduce this plan.

centre with most of the Highlanders further up the mountain on the left and a smaller division south of the river. Wightman reached the rebel position on 10 June and by late afternoon the battle had started.

The Government troops attacked first on their left to the south of the river, forcing the rebels to retreat across to the north. Then they attacked the rebels' left flank forcing another withdrawal, and then all forces were concentrated on the centre. The battle lasted about three hours, with the Spaniards retreating gradually to the top of the mountain. The Jacobite leaders, realising that their cause was lost, advised the Highlanders to disperse and the Spaniards to surrender. The mountain was re-named Sgurr nan Spainteach in their memory.

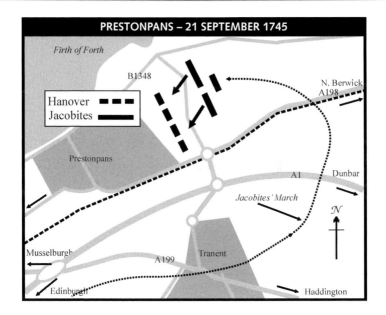

PRESTONPANS – 21 SEPTEMBER 1745

OS: NT403744

The battlefield is north of Tranent (on the A1) and just north of the railway line running from Edinburgh to North Berwick. The road from Tranent to Cockenzie runs through the heart of the site with the Jacobite forces lined up on one side, and the Hanoverians on the other.

Prince Charles Edward Stuart, the 'Young Pretender', landed in Scotland in July 1745, and set about raising the clans. On 19 August at Glenfinnan he raised his standard, signalling the start of the fourth and last Jacobite rising. The clans were reluctant at first to follow yet another Stuart, but sufficient heeded his call to arms to allow him to march south. General Sir John Cope (insultingly called by the Jacobites 'General of the Usurper's Army'), commander of the garrison in Scotland, reacted to this by marching his small force of 3,000 to meet Charles.

Cope headed towards Fort Augustus, but missed Charles who was then able to enter Edinburgh to acclaim. Cope then had to ship his army from Aberdeen to Dunbar. When the Jacobites received this news, they marched out of Edinburgh to face the Hanoverians and the two armies sighted each other just north of the village of Tranent on 20 September. The Hanoverians, facing the south, were protected to their front by marshy ground and had the sea at their backs.

The memorial to the Battle of Prestonpans beside the B1361 west of the junction with the A198.

During the night of 20/21 September, the Jacobites continued marching eastwards past Tranent and circled round their opponents, eventually lining up facing west towards Edinburgh. The Hanoverians wheeled to match their lines, so that they were now facing east.

The Jacobites had needed to cross a bog by a ford, and by so doing had unintentionally split their front line leaving a gap in the middle. Their reserves struggled to catch up and fill this gap, but the two wings charged the Hanoverians who broke within a few minutes. Most of the Hanoverian dead were killed in the pursuit rather than the battle itself, which lasted but ten minutes.

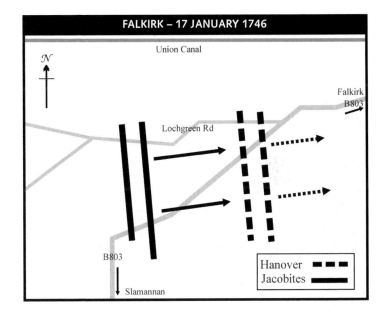

FALKIRK – 17 JANUARY 1746

Union Canal

Falkirk
B803

Lochgreen Rd

B803

Slamannan

Hanover ▬ ▬ ▬
Jacobites ▬▬▬

OS: NS875791

The battlefield is across the B803 about 1km south-west of Falkirk, where the B803, the Union Canal and the railway converge. The Jacobite line stretched from Greenbank Farm in the north to the Glen Burn. There is a memorial to the west behind the Jacobite lines.

After Prestonpans, Prince Charles turned again towards the south. He took Carlisle on 15 November and reached as far south as Derby. With news of three armies now ranged against him, the decision was made to return to Scotland on 6 December. Once over the border, reinforcements came quickly, and Prince Charles attacked Stirling Castle.

The Hanoverians, under General Henry Hawley, marched out of Edinburgh towards Stirling to relieve the castle, and the Jacobites marched south to meet this threat. Prince Charles sent a small diversionary force under Lord John Drummond on the direct road to Falkirk from Bannockburn, while he led his main force to Falkirk Muir, south-west of Falkirk. There, in a rainstorm, they met the Hanoverian force.

Before their infantry had reached their position, the Hanoverian dragoons made an initial charge on their left, but this was repulsed with heavy losses by musket fire. A follow-up charge by the Highlanders made the Hanoverian dragoons turn and flee, careering into their own left wing of infantry and causing it to disperse. The

Monument to the Battle of Falkirk. It stands between Lochgreen Road and Greenbank Road.

Highland centre now also charged causing the Hanoverian centre to crumble. The Hanoverian right wing, however, held firm. It was protected by a ravine from a charge, and it now wheeled and attacked the Highland left from the side.

Drummond by now had also reached the battlefield, becoming a reserve force. He now attacked the Hanoverian right wing, breaking its resistance and driving it from the field. The battle had lasted for about twenty minutes.

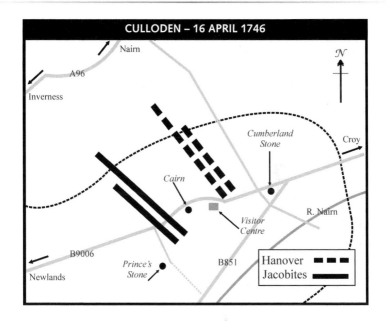

CULLODEN – 16 APRIL 1746

OS: NH741451

Culloden Muir is about 5km east of Inverness. The B9006 cuts through the battlefield and the Scottish National Trust Battlefield Information Centre is on this road. Where the B9006 meets the B851, there is the Cumberland Stone, and Bonnie Prince Charlie's Stone is about 1.5km south-west of this point.

Having defeated General Henry Hawley at Falkirk, Charles now returned to the siege of Stirling Castle. By 30 January, William, Duke of Cumberland, the younger son of George II, had reached Edinburgh and the Jacobite Council advised a retreat to Inverness. By 21 February this was achieved, and Charles tried to consolidate his position. Cumberland moved his base to Aberdeen, and by April began to advance towards Inverness, reaching Nairn on the 15th.

Prince Charles had drawn up in a defensive position at Culloden to the west of Inverness, much against the advice of Lord George Murray who preferred rough, broken terrain as opposed to the open moorland at Culloden because he feared the Hanoverian cavalry and artillery. On the night of 15/16 April, Charles decided to make a night attack against Cumberland's camp at Nairn.

He led his army through the night towards Nairn, but with many of his soldiers falling out because of hunger and exhaustion, Murray called off the attack and ordered a retreat despite Charles's accusation of betrayal. The Jacobites now had to return to their original position,

The Cumberland Stone. It is at the junction of the B9006 and the B851.

tired, hungry and dispirited. Cumberland determined to make the Jacobites pay for this reckless decision, and, on the morning of 16 April, immediately moved to the attack himself and faced Charles at the original position at Culloden.

The opening shots were made by the Jacobite artillery, but this was ineffective. The reply by the Hanoverians was devastating, tearing huge gaps in the ranks of the clansmen. No order to charge was given until the Hanoverians started firing grapeshot, and this was too much to bear without retaliation. The Highlanders charged and were mown down, this time by musket fire. When some of the clansmen broke through Cumberland's front line they were met by his second line and were trapped between the two lines of fire. Others started an orderly retreat but now Cumberland's cavalry charged home and turned the retreat into a rout.

WILLIAM THE CONQUEROR

Before William, Duke of Normandy, won the Battle of Hastings in 1066, he was already known as 'The Conqueror' due to his military capability. As a young man his favourite companion was his English cousin Edward, later known as 'The Confessor', who had been exiled to the Normandy court during the reign of King Canute. Edward was full of admiration for everything Norman, and, according to William, when he visited the English court, the celibate Edward declared him to be his successor.

In 1064 Harold Godwineson, who held the Earldom of Wessex, was brought to William's court after he had been shipwrecked off the Normandy coast. There he was induced to vow to support William's claim to the English throne when the time came. He then found he had been tricked into swearing over holy relics, thus giving the vow religious significance.

When Edward the Confessor died in January 1066 Harold was declared king by the Witan, the council that advised Anglo-Saxon kings, despite the fact that he was without royal blood. He was enthroned immediately.

When the news of this reached William in Normandy he resolved to invade England but his problem was that Harold's kingdom was larger and more powerful than Normandy, and he did not have enough troops for the campaign. He therefore wrote to Pope Alexander II claiming Harold had usurped the throne promised to him by the sainted Edward and in doing so had broken a vow made before God.

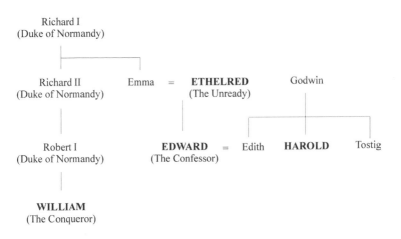

The Pope endorsed his cause and sent him a holy banner which in effect turned William's forthcoming campaign into a crusade, with German, French, Flemish and Italian adventurers joining William's army. With 5,000 knights under his command he crossed the Channel to Pevensey where prefabricated wooden forts brought over from France in sections were erected. Here he waited for Harold to march on him. On 14 October 1066 the battle was joined, Harold was slain and William became master of England, being crowned in Westminster Abbey on Christmas Day.

While in popular fiction William was often portrayed as a foreign invader who seized a throne to which he had no right, he was related to the last Saxon king. His son William II had an even closer tie, William's queen, Matilda, being descended from Alfred the Great.

The Battle of Hastings was the most significant battle to be fought on British soil, changing the structure of the country forever. As a consequence of William's victory, Norman customs and institutions, including administrative and legal systems, were introduced. The authority of the Church increased. Great cathedrals and mighty castles were built that remain objects of admiration to this day. Military organisation ensured that foreign raiders such as the Vikings would no longer be a threat. The feudal system was established and the first great survey of England – the Domesday Book – was carried out.

Memorial at St Valery sur Somme to the departure of William the Conqueror for England.

APPENDIX 2
ROYAL FAMILY TREE
From William the Conqueror to Edward III

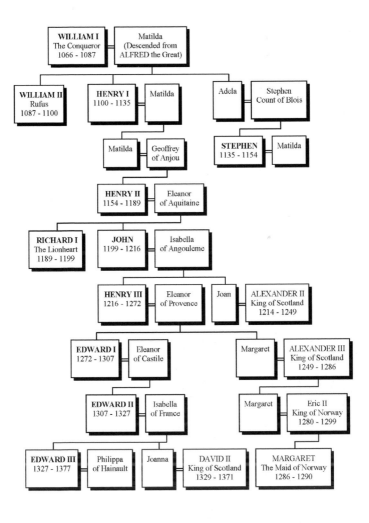

ROYAL FAMILY TREE

The Houses of Lancaster and York

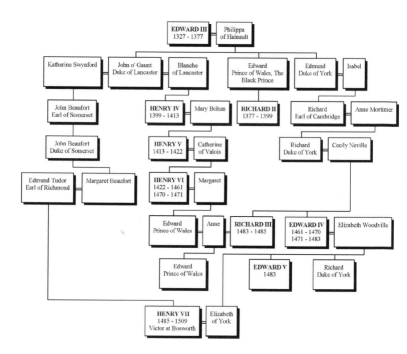

ROYAL FAMILY TREE

The Stuart Claim

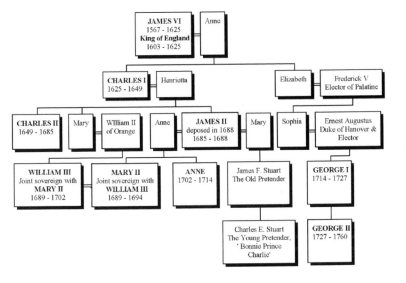

LIST OF BATTLES BY COUNTY

Aberdeenshire

Aberdeen	1644
Alford	1645

Angus

Dunnichen Moss	685

Berkshire (West)

Ashdown	871
Newbury (1)	1643
Newbury (2)	1644

Cheshire

Nantwich	1644
Rowton Heath	1645

Cornwall

Braddock Down	1643
Stratton	1643

Cumbria

Solway Moss	1542

Durham

Neville's Cross	1346

Essex

Ashingdon	1016
Maldon	991

Falkirk

Falkirk	1298
Falkirk	1746

Gloucestershire

Deorham	577
Lansdown	1643
Stow-on-the-Wold	1646
Tewkesbury	1471

Hampshire

Cheriton	1644

Herefordshire

Mortimer's Cross	1461

Hertfordshire

Barnet	1471
St Albans (1)	1455
St Albans (2)	1461

Highland

Auldearn	1645
Culloden	1746
Glen Shiel	1719
Inverlochy	1645

Republic of Ireland

Boyne	1690

Lanarkshire (North)

Kilsyth	1645

Leicestershire

Bosworth	1485

Lincolnshire

Winceby	1643

Lothian (East)

Dunbar	1296
Dunbar	1650
Pinkie	1547
Prestonpans	1745

Northamptonshire

Naseby	1645
Northampton	1460

Northumberland

Alnwick	1093
Halidon Hill	1333
Heavenfield	633
Hedgeley Moor	1464
Hexham	1464
Homildon Hill	1402
Flodden	1513
Otterburn	1388

Nottinghamshire

Stoke Field	1487

Oxfordshire

Chalgrove	1643
Edgcote	1469

Perth and Kinross

Killiecrankie	1689

Powys

Pilleth	1402

Scottish Borders

Ancrum Moor	1545

Shropshire

Ludford Bridge	1459
Shrewsbury	1403

Somerset

Langport	1645
Sedgemoor	1685

Staffordshire

Blore Heath	1459
Hopton Heath	1643

Stirling

Bannockburn	1314
Sheriffmuir	1715
Stirling Bridge	1297

Sussex (East)

Hastings	1066
Lewes	1264

Tyne and Wear

Newburn Ford	1640

Warwickshire

Cropredy Bridge	1644
Edgehill	1642

Wiltshire

Badon	c.500
Edington	878
Roundway Down	1643

Worcestershire

Evesham	1265
Powick Bridge	1642
Worcester	1651

Yorkshire (East Riding)

Fulford	1066
Stamford Bridge	1066

Yorkshire (North)

Boroughbridge	1322
Marston Moor	1644
Myton	1319
Standard	1138
Towton	1461

Yorkshire (West)

Adwalton Moor	1643
Wakefield	1460

INDEX